VOLUME THREE

WILHELM MEISTER'S YEARS OF APPRENTICESHIP

VOLUME THREE

WILHELM MEISTER'S YEARS OF APPRENTICESHIP

Wilhelm Meisters Lehrjahre

Books 7–8
by

Johann Wolfgang von Goethe

Translated by
H. M. Waidson

JOHN CALDER · LONDON
RIVERRUN PRESS · DALLAS

This translation from the German first published
1979 in Great Britain by
John Calder (Publishers) Ltd.,
18 Brewer Street, London W1R 4AS
and 1980 in the U.S.A. by
riverrun press Inc.,
Suite 247, 2800 Ruth Street,
Dallas, Texas 75201

© John Calder (Publishers) Ltd., 1979

British Library Cataloguing in Publication Data

Goethe, Johann Wolfgang von
Wilhelm Meister's years of apprenticeship.
Vol. 3
I. Title
833'.6   PT2027.W5   79-41173

ISBN 0-7145-3702-0

Typeset in 10pt Plantin by Blackburn Times Press Ltd., Blackburn.
Printed in Great Britain by Whitstable Litho Ltd,
Whitstable, Kent.

CONTENTS

WILHELM MEISTER'S YEARS OF APPRENTICESHIP

BOOK SEVEN

Chapter One

Spring had appeared in its full magnificence; an untimely storm that had been threatening all day broke turbulently on the heights, the rain moved over the countryside, the sun came out again in its radiance, and against the grey background the splendid rainbow became visible. Wilhelm was riding towards it and looked at it with melancholy. 'Oh!' he said to himself, 'is it true that the most beautiful colours of life only appear to us against a dark background? And that drops have to fall, if we are to be delighted? A bright day is like one that is overcast if we look at it without emotion, and what can move us if not the quiet hope that the inborn inclination of our heart may not remain without an object? We are moved by the story of every good deed and by the contemplation of every harmonious object; here we feel that we are not entirely on alien ground, we believe that we are closer to a home to which our best and innermost self impatiently aspires.'

In the meantime he was joined by a walker whose firm foot-steps kept pace with the horse, and who after some trivial remarks, said to the rider: 'If I am not mistaken, I must have seen you somewhere before.'

'I remember you too,' Wilhelm replied, 'didn't we have a merry boat trip together?' 'Quite right!' the other man answered.

Wilhelm looked at him more closely and after a period of silence he said: 'I don't know what sort of change has taken place in you; on that occasion I took you for a Lutheran country clergy-man, and now you look to me more like a Catholic one.'

'At least you are not deceiving yourself today,' the other man said, taking off his hat and revealing his tonsure. 'What has happened to the company you were with? Did you stay long with these people?'

'Longer than reasonable; for unfortunately when I think back to the time that I spent with them, I feel that I am looking into a void; I have retained nothing of this time.'

'You are mistaken; everything that happens to us leaves some traces, everything imperceptibly contributes to our development;

but it is dangerous to try to account for this to ourselves. In the process we either become arrogant and lackadaisical or else downcast and faint-hearted, and both are destructive as regards the future. The safest thing always is to pursue only what is nearest, and within grasp, and that now means,' he continued with a smile, 'that we make haste to find accommodation.'

Wilhelm asked how much further it was to Lothario's estate; the other man replied that it was beyond the hill. 'Perhaps I shall meet you there,' he continued, 'there is just something else I have to attend to in the neighbourhood. Goodbye for now!' And with these words he took a steep path which seemed to lead more quickly over the hill.

'Indeed he is right!' Wilhelm said to himself, as he rode on: 'One should think of what is nearest, and for me at present no doubt nothing is closer then the sad mission which I am to carry out. Let us see whether I can still recall the speech which is to put the cruel friend to shame.'

He then began to recite this masterpiece to himself; he did not forget a single syllable either, and the more his memory stood him in good stead, the more his passion and courage grew. Aurelia's sufferings and death were vividly present before his mind.

'Spirit of my friend!' he exclaimed, 'hover about me! And if it is possible for you, give me a sign to say that you have been placated and reconciled!'

In the course of these words and thoughts he had reached the brow of the hill and saw on its slope on the other side a strange building, which he at once took to be Lothario's dwelling-place. An old, irregularly built castle, with some towers and gables, seemed to have been its original design; but the new buildings which had been erected in part nearby, in part at some distance and which were linked with the main building by galleries and covered ways, were even more irregular. All outward symmetry, all architectural appearance seemed to have been sacrificed to the needs of interior comfort. There were no traces of ramparts and moat to be seen, nor of pleasure-gardens and large avenues. A vegetable-garden and orchard came up close to the buildings, and small serviceable gardens had been laid out even in the intervening spaces. A cheerful little village lay some distance off; gardens and fields appeared to be in perfect condition.

Preoccupied with his own passionate thoughts, Wilhelm rode on without thinking much about what he saw, left his horse at an inn and hurried, not without emotion, towards the castle.

An old manservant received him at the door and informed him in a very good-natured way that he would hardly be able to see the master today; the master had many letters to write and had already refused admittance to a number of his tradesmen. Wilhelm became more insistent, and in the end the old man had to give way and announce him. He came back and escorted Wilhelm into a large old assembly room. There he asked him to be patient, because the master might perhaps still keep him waiting for a time. Wilhelm paced restlessly up and down, and cast some glances at the knights and ladies whose ancient portraits hung on the walls; he repeated the opening of his speech, and in the presence of these suits of armour and ruffs it seemed to him more than ever in place. Whenever he heard any slight noise he struck an attitude in order to receive his antagonist with dignity, firstly to hand over the letter to him and then to fall upon him with the weapons of reproach.

Misled several times already, he was really beginning to be annoyed and upset when a handsome man in boots and wearing a simple overcoat at last appeared from a side-door. 'What good tidings are you bringing me?' he said to Wilhelm in a friendly voice, 'excuse me for keeping you waiting.'

While he was speaking he folded up a letter that he was holding in his hand. Not without embarrassment Wilhelm handed to him Aurelia's missive and said: 'I am bringing the last words of a friend which you will not be able to read without being moved.'

Lothario took the letter and at once went back to the room where, as Wilhelm could very well see through the open door, he first sealed up some further letters and wrote their addresses, and then opened and read Aurelia's letter. He appeared to have read the note through several times, and although Wilhelm felt that his solemn speech did not rightly fit in with the spontaneous reception he had had, he none the less pulled himself together and was about to begin his message when a concealed door in the private room opened and the clergyman entered.

'I've just received the strangest dispatch in the world,' Lothario called to him; 'excuse me,' he went on, turning to Wilhelm, 'if I am not at the moment in the mood for continuing a conversation with you. You must spend the night here! And you will look after our guest, Abbé, and see that he wants for nothing.'

With these words he bowed towards Wilhelm, the Abbé took our friend's hand, though the latter did not follow without resistance.

They went silently along strange corridors and arrived at a very pleasant room. The clergyman ushered him in and left him there without further apology. Soon after a cheerful boy appeared who announced himself to Wilhelm as his servant and brought in the evening meal; while he was acting as waiter he volunteered information about the routine of the household, how one usually took breakfast, dined, worked and amused oneself, and in particular he had much to say in praise of Lothario.

Agreeable though the boy was, Wilhelm tried to get rid of him soon. He wanted to be alone, for he felt extremely weighed down and uneasy. He reproached himself for having carried out his intention so badly and for having only partly fulfilled his mission. Sometimes he resolved to make good next morning what had been neglected, at other times he was aware that the presence of Lothario was rousing quite different feelings in him. The house where he now was seemed to him so extraordinary that he could not adjust himself to his position. He wished to undress, and opened his case; together with his night things he brought out the Ghost's veil which Mignon had put in. The sight of it increased his sadness of mood. '"Take flight! Young man, take flight!"' he exclaimed, 'What are the mystic words supposed to mean? Take flight from what? Take flight where to? The Ghost would have done much better to call to me: "Go back to yourself!"' He looked at the framed English prints which were hanging on the wall; indifferently his glance passed over most of them, but finally he discovered a portrait of a shipwreck: a father with his beautiful daughters was awaiting death from the invading waves. The one female figure seemed to resemble that Amazon; an inexpressible pity seized our friend, he felt an irresistible need to ease his heartfelt emotions, tears welled to his eyes, and he could not recover before sleep overcame him.

Towards morning he was haunted by strange dreams. He was in a garden which he had often visited as a boy, and was pleased to see once more the familiar avenues, hedges and flower-beds; he met Mariane, he talked affectionately to her and without recollection of any past misunderstanding. Immediately afterwards his father came up to him, wearing indoor-clothing; and with an intimately confiding expression that was unlike him, he told his son to fetch two chairs from the summer-house, took Mariane by the hand and escorted her to an arbour.

Wilhelm hurried to the room overlooking the garden, but found it quite empty except for Aurelia standing at the far window; he made as if to speak to her, but she remained unmoving, and although he went up to her, he could not see her face. He looked out of the window and saw, in a strange garden, a gathering of many people, some of whom he recognized at once. Madame Melina was sitting under a tree, playing with a rose she held in her hand; Laertes was standing by her, counting gold coins from one hand to another. Mignon and Felix were lying in the grass, the former stretched out on her back, the latter with his face downward. Philine appeared and clapped her hands above the children, Mignon stayed without moving, Felix leapt up and fled from Philine. At first he was laughing as he ran with Philine chasing him, then he cried with fear as the Harpist pursued him with long slow steps. The child ran straight off towards a pool; Wilhelm hurried after him, but was too late, the child was lying in the water! Wilhelm was as if rooted to the spot. He now saw the beautiful Amazon on the other side of the pool; she stretched out her hand towards the child and went along the bank in his direction, the child sped through the water moving directly towards her finger and followed her as she walked, finally she stretched out her hand to him and pulled him out of the pool. Meanwhile Wilhelm had come closer, the child was completely on fire, and fiery drops were falling from him. Wilhelm became more fearful, but the Amazon quickly removed a white veil from her head and covered the child with it. The fire was at once extinguished. When she lifted the veil, two boys leapt forth who played mischievously together this way and that, while Wilhelm went hand in hand with the Amazon through the garden, and saw in the distance his father and Mariane walking in the avenue which seemed to surround the whole garden with high trees. He directed his way towards the two of them and was cutting across the garden with his beautiful companion when all at once fairhaired Friedrich stepped in their path and held them up with much laughter and all kinds of pranks. For all that they wanted to continue on their way; then he ran off towards that distant couple; his father and Mariane seemed to be taking flight from him, he only ran the faster, and Wilhelm saw them gliding away down the avenue, almost flying. Instinct and inclination invited him to come to their help, but the Amazon's hand held him back. How gladly he let himself be held! He awakened with this mixed feeling and found his room already illuminated by the bright sun.

Chapter Two

The boy invited Wilhelm to breakfast; the latter found the Abbé already in the assembly room; Lothario, it was said, had gone out riding; the Abbé was not very talkative and seemed rather to be reflective; he asked about Aurelia's death and listened sympathetically to Wilhelm's narrative. 'Alas,' he exclaimed, 'whoever is conscious of the infinite machinations that nature and art must carry out before a cultivated man emerges, whoever participates to his limits in the education of his fellow men might well despair when he sees how criminally man often destroys himself and equally often is placed in the position, whether guiltily or innocently, of being destroyed. When I consider this, life itself seems to me such a chance gift, that I should be glad to praise as happy any man who does not value it more highly than is reasonable.'

He had scarcely finished speaking when the door was flung violently open and a young woman burst in, pushing aside the old manservant who was intercepting her. She hurried straight up to the Abbé and caught him by the arm, but could scarcely utter her few words for weeping: 'Where is he? Where have you put him? It is a frightful betrayal! Just admit! I know what is going on! I want to go after him! I want to know where he is.'

'Calm yourself my child,' the Abbé said with assumed composure, 'Go to your room, you will hear everything, only you must be able to listen when I am to tell you about it.' He offered her his hand, with a view to leading her away. 'I shan't go to my room,' she cried out, 'I hate the walls between which you have already kept me prisoner for so long! And yet I've found out everything, the colonel has challenged him to a duel, he has gone off on horseback to seek out his opponent, and possibly now, just at this very minute—it seemed to me a number of times that I could hear shooting. Have the horses harnessed and come with me, else I shall fill the house and whole village with my screaming.'

She rushed to the window amid the most impassioned tears, the Abbé held her back and tried in vain to calm her down.

There was the sound of an approaching carriage, she wrenched open the window: 'He's dead,' she shouted, 'there, they're bringing him.'—'He is getting out!' the Abbé said. 'You see, he's alive.' —'He's wounded,' she replied vehemently, 'otherwise he'd come on horseback! They're leading him! He's seriously wounded!' She ran out by the door and down the steps, the Abbé hurried after her, and Wilhelm followed them; he saw how the beautiful woman encountered her lover as he was approaching.

Lothario was leaning on his companion, whom Wilhelm immediately recognized as his old patron Jarno, spoke in an affectionate and friendly way to the inconsolable woman, and came slowly up the steps as he supported himself against her as well; he greeted Wilhelm and was led to his private room.

Not long after Jarno came out again and went up to Wilhelm, saying: 'It seems that you are predestined to find actors and theatre wherever you go; we are just now caught up in a drama that is not all that amusing.'

'I am glad to meet you again at this extraordinary moment,' Wilhelm replied; 'I am surprised and shocked, and your presence at once makes me quiet and composed. Tell me, is there danger? Has the Baron been seriously wounded?'—'I don't think so,' Jarno rejoined.

After a time the young surgeon came out of the private room. 'What do you say now?' Jarno called to him. 'It's very dangerous,' he added, putting some implements back into his leather bag.

Wilhelm looked at the ribbon which was hanging down from the bag; he thought he recognized it. Vivid, contrasting colours, an unusual pattern, and gold and silver in strange shapes distinguished this ribbon from all other ribbons in the world. Wilhelm was convinced that what he saw was the instrument case of the old surgeon who had bound his wounds in that forest, and the hope of again finding a trace of his Amazon after such a long time lit up like a flame within him.

'Where did you get that case?' he exclaimed. 'Who did it belong to before yourself? Please, do tell me.'—'I bought it at an auction,' the other man replied, 'what do you care as to who owned it previously?' Having spoken these words, he went off, and Jarno said: 'If only this young man could be trusted to speak one word of truth.'—'So he didn't pick up this case at an auction?' Wilhelm rejoined.—'No more than Lothario is in any kind of danger,' Jarno answered.

Wilhelm was immersed in various musings when Jarno asked him how he had fared recently. Wilhelm outlined his story and when finally he had recounted Aurelia's death and his mission, Jarno exclaimed: 'It really is strange, very strange!'

The Abbé came out of the other room, beckoned to Jarno to enter in his place, and said to Wilhelm: 'The Baron would like to invite you to stay here, to swell the number of the company for a few days and to contribute to his entertainment in the present circumstances. If you need to send any messages to your friends, any letter you may write will be dealt with at once, and I must tell you something that is in fact no secret, so that you may understand this strange incident which you have witnessed. The Baron had a little adventure with a lady which attracted more attention than was proper because she wanted to enjoy all too keenly the triumph of having snatched him from a rival. Unfortunately, after a certain time he did not find the same pleasure with her, and he avoided her; only with her passionate temperament she found it impossible to bear her fate with equanimity. In the course of a ball it came to an open break, she believed that she had been extremely insulted and wished to be avenged; no cavalier could be found to champion her cause until finally her husband, from whom she had been separated for a long time, heard about the matter and took up her cause, challenged the Baron and today wounded him; but things have even gone worse with the Colonel, I understand.'

From this moment on our friend was treated in the house as if he belonged to the family.

Chapter Three

They had read aloud a number of times to the sick man. Wilhelm was happy to perform this little service. Lydia would not leave the bedside, her care for the wounded man absorbed her attention above all else, but today even Lothario seemed distracted, indeed he asked for the reading to be stopped.

'Today I feel so keenly how foolishly man lets his time pass by!' he said. 'How many resolutions I have made, how much I have worked out in my mind, and how do we not hesitate with our best intentions! I have studied the suggestions for the changes which I wish to make on my estates, and I can say that for this reason I am very happy that the bullet did not take a more dangerous path.'

Lydia looked at him tenderly, indeed with tears in her eyes, as if she wanted to ask whether she and his friends could not also make claims to share in this enjoyment of life. Jarno, on the other hand, replied: 'Changes such as you propose need first to be considered fairly from all points of view before a decision is made.'

'Lengthy considerations,' Lothario said, 'usually show that we do not see clearly the point in question, overhasty actions show that we are not aware of the point at all. I perceive very clearly that in many contexts relating to the management of my estates I cannot dispense with the service of my farmers and that I must insist promptly and strictly upon certain rights; but I also see that other powers are admittedly advantageous to me, but not absolutely indispensable, so that I can hand over some of them to my people. We don't always lose when we do without. Am I not making much better use of my land than my father did? Shall I not be able to increase my income even further? And am I to enjoy this increasing advantage on my own? Am I not to grant the man who works with me and for me advantages also in his sphere which extended knowledge and the passing of time offer us?'

'Well, that's the way people are!' cried Jarno, 'and I don't reprove myself when I catch myself out in this oddity; man wants to seize everything for himself, in order just to be able to dispose of it as he fancies; money that he doesn't spend himself seldom seems to him to be well spent.'

'Oh, indeed!' Lothario replied, 'we could do without much of the capital, if we dealt with the interest in a less arbitrary manner.'

'The only thing that I have to recall to you,' said Jarno, 'and why I can't advise you to make these particular alterations now, which will cause you losses, at least for the time being, is that you yourself still have debts whose payment hems you in. I would advise postponing your plan until you are completely in the clear.'

'And meanwhile leaving it to a bullet or a slate from a roof to decide whether the results of my life and work should be destroyed for ever! Oh, my friend!' Lothario continued, 'that is one of the main failings of cultured people, that they tend to direct all their energies to an idea, but little or none to an object. Why have I got into debt? Why have I quarrelled with my uncle and left my brothers and sisters to themselves for so long, if not for an idea? I believed that I could be effective in America, I believed I could be useful and necessary across the sea; if an activity were not surrounded by a thousand dangers, it did not seem to me to be significant or worthwhile. How differently I see things now, and how valuable and dear to me what is close at hand has become.'

'I can certainly remember the letter which I received from over the sea,' Jarno replied. 'You wrote to me: "I shall return and say in my own house, in my orchard and amid my own people: *Here or nowhere is America!*"'

'Yes, my friend, and I keep on repeating these words, though at the same time I reproach myself for not being as active here as I was there. For a certain type of smooth running, continuous present we need only common sense, with the result that we no longer see the extraordinary thing that any routine day demands of us, and if we do recognize it, we find a thousand excuses for not doing it. A sensible person means much for himself, but he means little for the whole enterprise.'

'Let's not take too familiar an approach to common sense,' said Jarno, 'and let us admit that the extraordinary things that happen are mostly foolish.'

'Yes, and what is more, just because people do extraordinary things outside the course of events. Thus my brother-in-law gives his fortune, as far as he is able to dispose of it, to the Moravian Brethren and believes that he is furthering his soul's salvation by this; if he had given up a small part of his income, he would have been able to make many people happy and to create a heaven upon earth for them. Our sacrifices are seldom matters of activity, we immediately give up what we give away. When we renounce what we own, it is not with determination but in despair. Just recently, I admit, I have kept on thinking of the Count, and I am firmly determined to do as a matter of conviction what he was driven to by an anxious delusion; I won't wait for my health to recover. Here are the papers, all they need is to be tidied up. Get the magistrate to work at them, our guest will help you too, you know as well as I do what is needed, and I will stay here, whether I recover or die, and cry: *Here or nowhere is Herrnhut!*'

When Lydia heard her friend talk about dying, she fell down by his bedside, clung to his arms and wept bitterly. The surgeon came in, Jarno gave Wilhelm the papers and urged Lydia to leave.

'For heaven's sake,' cried Wilhelm, when they were alone in the room, 'what's this about the Count? Which Count is it who is taking up with the Moravian community?'

'Someone you know very well,' Jarno replied. 'You are the ghost that is chasing him into the arms of piety, you are the villain who is putting his nice wife into a position where she finds it tolerable to follow her husband.'

'And she is Lothario's sister?' cried Wilhelm.

'No other.'

'And Lothario knows——?'

'Everything.'

'Oh, let me disappear!' Wilhelm exclaimed, 'how can I appear before him? What can he say?'

'That nobody should pick up a stone to cast at another, and that nobody should prepare long speeches in order to put other people to shame, unless he wants to deliver the speeches in front of the mirror.'

'You know that too?'

'Like many other things,' Jarno replied with a smile; 'but this time,' he continued, 'I shan't let you escape as easily as before, and you also no longer have to be afraid of my recruitment fee. I am not a soldier any more, and even as a soldier I ought not to have saddled you with this suspicion. A lot has changed since that last time I saw you. After the death of my prince, my only friend and benefactor, I tore myself away from the court society and from all relationships connected with it. I used to be glad to sponsor what was sensible, did not keep silent when I found something silly, and people always had something to say about my restless brain and my malicious tongue. The crowd fear nothing more than good sense; if they understood what is to be feared, they should be afraid of stupidity; but good sense is uncomfortable, and must be pushed to one side, whereas stupidity is only harmful, and that's something we can wait for. But that may pass, I've enough to live on, and you shall hear further about my plan. You are to have a part in it, if you wish; but tell me, how have things gone with you? I see that you too have changed, I can sense it. How are things with regard to your former fancy of producing something beautiful and good in association with gypsies?'

'I've been punished enough!' Wilhelm exclaimed; 'don't remind me where I have come from and where I am going to. There's a lot of talk about the theatre, but no one who has not himself worked there can have any notion about it. How completely these people are ignorant of themselves, how they get on with the business without thinking about what they are doing, and the unbounded nature of their demands, these are matters which other people can have no idea of. Not only does each wish to be the first, but he also wants to be the only one, each one would like to exclude all the rest and does not see that he scarcely accomplishes anything working with them together; each imagines himself to be wonderfully original and is incapable of finding anything in himself apart from routine; but at the same time there is constant restlessness in search of something new. How passionately they conflict with one another! And only the pettiest self-love and most limited selfishness have the effect of binding them together. There is no talk at all of mutually considerate behaviour; a never-ending mistrust is kept going by secret malice and shameful talk; if you don't live in a loose way, you are just silly. Each lays claim to the most unqualified respect, each is sensitive to the slightest reproof. He already knew better about all that! And why then did he always do the opposite? Always needy and always untrusting, it seems as if they would be afraid of nothing so much as reason and good taste and would try to preserve nothing so much as the sovereign prerogative of their personal caprice.'

Wilhelm drew breath in order to continue further with his litany, when an immoderate outburst of laughter from Jarno interrupted him. 'The poor actors!' he exclaimed, flung himself into a chair and went on laughing; 'the poor, good actors! Do you realize, my friend,' he continued after he had recovered himself to some extent, 'that what you have described is not the theatre, but the world of society, and that I could find you enough characters and actions from all social classes to justify your hard brush-strokes? Excuse me, I shall have to laugh again, to think that you believed that these fine qualities were only to be found among actors.'

Wilhelm took hold of himself, for Jarno's immoderate and untimely laughter had really annoyed him. 'You cannot completely conceal your misanthropy, if you maintain that these faults are general.'

'And it bears witness to your unfamiliarity with the world that you ascribe to the theatre so much responsibility for these manifestations. In truth, I can pardon the actor for every fault that derives from self-deception and the desire to please; for unless he appears as something to himself and others, he is nothing. Appearances are his vocation, he must value highly the applause of the moment, for he receives no other reward; he must attempt to be outstanding, for that is why he is there.'

'You will allow me, from my point of view, at least to smile,' Wilhelm rejoined. 'I should never have believed that you could be so fair and indulgent.'

'No, by God! This is my fully considered, serious view. I forgive the actor all human failings, I forgive man for none of the actor's failings. Don't let me start my lamentations on this theme, they would sound more violent than your own.'

The surgeon came from the inner room, and when asked how the sick man was, he said in a lively, friendly way: 'Very well, I hope soon to see him fully restored to health.' He then hurried out to the larger room and did not wait for the question which Wilhelm, who was already opening his mouth, was about to ask again about the case and in a more insistent manner. The wish to hear something about his Amazon gave him confidence in Jarno; he revealed his position to him and asked him for his assistance. 'You know so much,' he said, 'should you not also be able to find this out as well?'

Jarno was thoughtful for a moment, then he said to his young friend: 'Be calm, and appear to know nothing further about the matter, we shall soon get on to the track of the beautiful lady. All that I am worried about now is Lothario's condition, the position is dangerous, I can tell that from the friendliness and the cheerful approach of the surgeon. I would have been glad to get Lydia away before now, for she is of no use here, but I don't know how to set about it. I am hoping that our old medical man will come this evening, and then we can discuss things further.'

Chapter Four

The medical man came; it was the kind old doctor whom we know already and to whom we owe the communication of the interesting manuscript. In the first place he was visiting the injured man and appeared to be not at all satisfied with his condition. Then he had a long conversation with Jarno, though they said nothing about this when they came to dine in the evening.

Wilhelm greeted him very cordially and inquired after his Harpist.—'We are still hopeful that we can set the unfortunate man to rights,' the doctor replied.—'This fellow has been a sad addition to your confined and strange life,' Jarno said. 'How has he been getting on recently? Do tell me.'

After Jarno's curiosity had been satisfied the doctor continued: 'I have never seen a mind in such an unusual state. For many years he did not make the slightest response to anything outside himself, in fact to anything at all; merely turned in upon himself, he contemplated his hollow, empty ego that seemed to him to be an immeasurable abyss. How moving it was when he spoke of this sad condition! "I see nothing before me and nothing behind me except an interminable night where I am in the most terrible isolation; no emotion is left except the feeling of my guilt, which none the less can only be seen in retrospect as a remote, misshapen ghost. But here there is no height, no depth, no going forward nor coming back; no words can express the sameness of this state. In my distress at this indifference I often call out 'ever more! ever more!' in impassioned tones, and these strange, incomprehensible words are bright and clear against the darkness of my condition. No gleams from a divinity appear to me in this night, I weep all my tears to myself and about myself. To me nothing is more terrible than friendship and love; for they alone tempt me to wish that these manifestations which surround me might be real. But these two ghosts also have only risen from the abyss in order to frighten me and in the end as well to rob me of the beloved consciousness of this monstrous existence."'

'You should hear him,' the doctor continued, 'when he relieves his heart in this way during periods when he is in a confiding mood; I have listened to him a number of times with the greatest emotion. When something forces itself upon his attention which compels him to admit for a moment that a certain length of time has passed, he seems as if surprised, and then he again rejects the way things have changed as a manifestation of appearances. One evening he sang a song about his grey hair; we all sat around him and were in tears.'

'Oh, do get it for me!' Wilhelm exclaimed.

'But haven't you found out anything about what he calls his crime, or the reason for his strange clothes, for his behaviour during the fire, or his rage against the child?'

'We can only approach closer to his fate through surmises; to ask him directly would be against our principles. Since we can observe that he has been brought up as a Catholic, we thought we might be able to bring him comfort through the confessional; but he disappears in a strange fashion every time that we try to take him to the priest. But I am willing to let you know our assumptions at least, so that I need not leave your wish to know something about him completely unsatisfied. He spent his youth in the ecclesiastical profession; this seems to be why he wants to retain his long robe and his beard. For most of his life he knew nothing of the joys of love. Only late in life may an aberrant relationship with a woman who was very closely related to him and her death in giving birth to an unfortunate creature have been the cause of unhinging his mind completely.

'His greatest delusion is that he brings misfortune everywhere and that his death will be brought about by an innocent child. At first he was afraid of Mignon, before he knew that she was a girl; now Felix has been arousing his fears, and as for all his misery he has an infinite love of life, this seems to have been the reason for his dislike of the child.'

'What hopes have you then for his recovery?' Wilhelm asked.

'There is slow progress,' the doctor replied, 'but still, he is not going back. He continues his particular occupations, and we have accustomed him to reading the newspapers, which he now always looks forward to very eagerly.'

'I am curious about his songs,' Jarno said.

'I shall be able to give you a number of them,' the doctor said.

'The clergyman's eldest son, who is used to taking down his father's sermons, has made note of many a verse without the old man noticing and has gradually put together a number of songs.'

Next morning Jarno came to Wilhelm and said to him: 'You must do us a favour; Lydia must be got out of the way for a time; the violence and, I may well say, the inconvenience of her love and passion are a hindrance to the Baron's recovery. His wound requires him to be quiet and composed, although with his strong constitution it is not dangerous. You have seen how Lydia tortures him with stormy attentions, with fears that she cannot suppress, and with never-ending tears, and—enough,' he added with a smile after a pause, 'the doctor expressly requires that she should leave the house for a time. We have caused her to imagine that a very good woman friend of hers is staying in the neighbourhood, is wanting to see her and is expecting her any moment. She has let herself be persuaded to go to the magistrate, who lives only two hours away from here. This man has been put in the picture and will express heartfelt regrets that Miss Theresa has just left; he will make it seem likely that it is still possible to catch her up. Lydia will hurry on after her, and if luck holds, she will be led on from one place to another. In the end, when she insists on turning back again, she will not be opposed; night must be called upon to help, the coachman is a clever fellow with whom it will be necessary to come to an agreement. You can sit with her in the coach, keep her entertained and manoeuvre the adventure.'

'You are giving me a strange and questionable mission,'Wilhelm replied; 'the presence of a faithful love that has been hurt is a matter for anxiety! And I myself am to be the instrument of this? It is the first time in my life that I shall have deceived anyone in this way: for I have always believed that it would take us too far, if we were once to start deceiving for the sake of what is good and useful.'

'But it's impossible to educate children except in this way,' Jarno put in.

'It may still be all right with children,' Wilhelm said, 'since we love them so tenderly and obviously make allowances for them; but in the case of people like ourselves, on whose behalf our heart does not call to us so loudly to exercise forbearance, it might often become dangerous. But don't believe that I am refusing the task on this account,' he continued after short reflection. 'I am quite happy to forget myself because of the respect which your intelligence arouses in me, because of the inclination which I feel towards your excellent friend, and because of my keen wish to assist in his recovery by whatever means are possible. It is not enough to be able to venture one's life for a friend, one must also, if need be, deny one's convictions for him. It is our obligation to sacrifice on his behalf our dearest passion and our fondest wishes. I will take on the mission, although I can already foresee the distress that I shall have to suffer from Lydia's tears and despair.'

'On the other hand, no slight recompense awaits you either,' Jarno rejoined, 'as you will meet Miss Theresa, a woman of a rare kind; she can put to shame a hundred men, and I should like to call her a true Amazon, while others go around in this ambivalent dress only as charming hermaphrodites.'

Wilhelm was taken aback; he hoped to find his Amazon again in Theresa, all the more so as Jarno, from whom he asked for some information, broke off abruptly and went away.

The new, near hope of seeing that revered and loved figure again aroused in him the strangest feelings. He now saw the mission which he had been given as an expressly providential piece of work, and the thought that he was about to remove by deceit a poor young girl from the object of her most sincere and impassioned love only went through his mind in passing, just as a bird's shadow flies away across the sunlit earth.

The carriage was at the door, Lydia hesitated to get in for a moment. 'Give your master my greetings again,' she said to the old servant. 'I shall be back before the evening.' Tears were in her eyes when she turned round once more as they were driving off. Then she turned to Wilhelm, pulled herself together and said: 'You will find in Miss Theresa a very interesting person. I wonder how she comes to be in this neighbourhood: for I expect you know that she and the Baron were passionately in love. In spite of the distance Lothario was often visiting her; at that time I was with Theresa, and it seemed as if they would only live for one another. But all at once it was shattered, without anyone being able to understand why. He had got to know me, and I don't deny that I cordially envied Theresa, that I scarcely concealed my attraction towards him, and that I did not repulse him when he seemed all at once to be choosing me instead of Theresa. I could not have wished for her to behave better towards me, although it must almost have seemed as if I had robbed her of such a highly prized lover. But how many tears and sorrows too has this love already cost me! At first we only met occasionally in secret at a third place, but I could not put up with this life for long; I was only happy, really happy, in his presence. When I was away from him my eyes were moist and my pulse-beat uneven. On one occasion he was away for several days, I was in despair, set out and surprised him here. He welcomed me affectionately, and if this wretched quarrel had not interfered, I should have been having a heavenly time; and I can't say what I have put up with since he has been in danger and suffering, and at this very moment I reproach myself very much for having been able to leave him for one day only.'

Wilhelm was about to inquire further about Theresa when they drove up to the magistrate's house; he came to the carriage and greatly regretted that Miss Theresa had already left. He offered the travellers breakfast, but at the same time said that they should be able to catch up with the coach in the next village. They decided to follow, and the coachman did not linger; they had already left some villages behind them without meeting anybody. Lydia now insisted on turning back; the coachman went on driving, as if he had not understood. Finally she demanded it with extreme vehemence; Wilhelm called to him and gave him the agreed signal. The coachman replied: 'We don't need to take the same way back; I know a more direct one which at the same time is much more comfortable.' He now drove to the side through a forest and over long stretches of pasture land. In the end when no familiar landmark showed itself, the coachman admitted that unfortunately he had lost his way, but that he would soon find it again, as he could see a village over there. Night came on, and the coachman played his part so skilfully that he was asking everywhere and nowhere waiting for a reply. Thus the journeying went on the whole night, Lydia did not shut an eye; in the moonlight she was finding resemblances everywhere, and they always disappeared again. In the morning the surroundings seemed familiar to her, but all the more unexpected. The carriage drew up in front of a small, charmingly constructed country house; a lady stepped out of the doorway and opened the carriage-door. Lydia stared at her, looked round, looked at her again and fainted in Wilhelm's arms.

Chapter Five

Wilhelm was conducted to a small attic room; the house was new and almost as small as it could possibly be, and very clean and tidy. He had not found his Amazon in Theresa, who had welcomed him and Lydia at the carriage; she was another person, vastly different from her. She was well-built without being tall, she moved about in very lively manner, and nothing that went on seemed to be hidden from her bright, blue, open eyes.

She came into Wilhelm's room and asked if he needed anything. 'Excuse me for putting you into a room that is still unpleasant from the smell of oil,' she said; 'my small house has just been finished, and you are inaugurating this little room which is intended for my guests. If only you were here for a more agreeable reason! Poor Lydia won't make things easy for us, and altogether you will have to make do; my cook has left me at just the wrong time, and a servant has crushed his hand. If needs be, I shall do everything myself, and in the end that would work out all right once one was adjusted to it. There is more trouble with servants than with anybody; nobody wishes to give service, not even to himself.'

She had various other things to say about a number of topics; in general she seemed to like talking. Wilhelm asked after Lydia, and whether he might not see the dear girl and make his apologies to her.

'At the moment that won't be effective as far as she is concerned,' Theresa replied, 'time forgives just as it consoles; in both cases words have little influence. Lydia does not wish to see you. "Don't let him come into my sight," she cried when I left her, "I feel like despairing of mankind! Such an honest face, such open behaviour and this secret malice!" Lothario is fully excused in her eyes; what is more, he says in a letter to the dear girl: "My friends persuaded me, my friends put pressure on me!" Lydia counts you among these too and condemns you along with the others.'

'She is honouring me too much when she reproaches me,' Wilhelm replied; 'as yet I may lay no claim to the friendship of this excellent man and on this occasion I am only an innocent instrument. I don't want to praise my action; enough, I could do it! There was talk of the health and life of a man whom I must esteem more highly than anyone I knew previously. Oh, what a man he is, Miss Theresa, and what people there are about him! I may well say that I took part in a conversation for the first time, and that for the first time the most particular meaning of my words was returned to me from the lips of another more abundantly and fully and in greater range; what I surmised became clear to me, and what I supposed I learnt to look at. Unfortunately this pleasure was interrupted firstly by all kinds of worries and fancies, and then by the unpleasant mission. I undertook it with submission: for I believed that I was obliged to pay my dues for entry to this fine group of people even with the sacrifice of my personal feeling.'

Theresa had been looking at her guest in a very friendly way while these words were being spoken. 'Oh how pleasing it is,' she exclaimed, 'to hear one's own convictions being uttered by another's lips! How we really become ourselves when someone else fully agrees with us. I too think of Lothario completely as you do; not everyone is prepared to do him justice; on the other hand all who know him well are enthusiastic about him, and the sorrowful feeling that is associated in my heart with his memory can't prevent me from thinking daily about him.' As she said this she heaved a sigh, and a beautiful tear gleamed in her right eye. 'Don't think,' she continued, 'that I am all that gentle and easily moved! It is only the eye that weeps. I had a small wart on my lower eye-lid, it has been successfully removed, but ever since my eye has been weak, and the slightest pretext causes tears to flow. This is where the little wart was, you can't see any trace of it any longer.'

He could see no trace, but looked into her eyes; they were as clear as crystal, he felt he was looking to the bottom of her soul.

'We have now spoken the password of our association,' she said; 'let us get to know each other as soon as possible. Man's story is his character. I will tell you what has happened in my life, treat me with the same trust and let us remain united even at a distance. The world is so empty if we only think of it as containing mountains, rivers and towns, but to know of someone here and there who is in agreement with us, and with whom we can go on living, even in silence, is needed to make the planet into an inhabited garden for us.'

She hastened away and promised to call for him soon to take a walk. Her presence had affected him very agreeably; he wanted to find out about her relationship with Lothario. He was summoned, she came from her room to meet him.

As they had to go down the narrow and rather steep staircase in single file, she said: 'All this could have been wider and more extensive, if I had been willing to listen to your generous friend's offer; but in order to remain worthy of him I must retain that about myself which made me so valuable to him. Where is the steward?' she asked as she arrived at the foot of the stairs. 'You must not think,' she went on, 'that I am so rich that I need a steward; I can indeed deal with the few fields of my little freehold on my own. The steward belongs to my new neighbour who has bought the lovely estate that I know so well; the good old man lies ill with gout, his people are new to this district, and I am glad to assist them to settle in.'

They took a walk through fields, meadows and some orchards. Theresa was everywhere giving the steward advice, she could give an account of every detail, and Wilhelm had reason enough to be astonished at her knowledge, her sureness and her skill in recommending what to do in each case. She did not linger anywhere, always hastening to the important points, and so the matter was soon settled. 'Give my greetings to your master,' she said as she was dismissing the man: 'I shall visit him as soon as possible and hope that he will be fully recovered. Now there I could also soon be rich and have many possessions,' she said with a smile, after he had gone; 'for my good neighbour would not be averse to offering me his hand.'

'The old man with gout?' Wilhelm cried: 'I don't know how at your age you could come to so desperate a decision.'—'I'm not at all tempted to do so either!' Theresa replied. 'Everyone is prosperous who knows how to manage what he has; it is a tiresome business to be the owner of many possessions when you don't know how to deal with them.'

Wilhelm showed his surprise at her knowledge of administraion.—'A distinct liking, early opportunity, an external motive and continuing occupation in a useful matter make even more things possible in this world,' Theresa rejoined, 'and when you learn what has been my inspiration you will no longer be taken aback by what seems to you a strange talent.'

When they reached her home again, she left him in her little garden, in which he could hardly turn round, so narrow were the paths and so abundantly full of plants all the ground was. He could not help smiling when he returned across the yard, for the firewood had been so tidily sawn, split and stacked that it seemed as if it were a part of the building, intended to lie there for ever. All containers stood neatly in their places, the little house had been painted red and white, and was gay in appearance. What can be achieved by craftsmanship which is unfamiliar with beautiful conditions but works with utility, durability and cheerfulness in mind seemed to have come together here. Food was brought to him in his room, and he had time enough to reflect. It struck his attention particularly that he was again making the acquaintance of a very interesting person who had a close relationship with Lothario. 'It is right,' he said to himself, 'that such an excellent man should also attract excellent women! How wide-ranging is the impact of manliness and dignity! If only others did not come off so very badly in the process! Yes, just confess your fears. If some day you do meet your Amazon again, this person above all persons, you will find her to be in spite of all your hopes and dreams, to your shame and humiliation, in the end—his fiancée.'

Chapter Six

Wilhelm had spent a restless afternoon not completely without boredom when his door opened towards evening and a young and charming huntsman entered with a greeting. 'Shall we go for a walk now?' the young person asked, and at that moment Wilhelm recognized Theresa by her beautiful eyes.

'Excuse this masquerade,' she began, 'for unfortunately it is only a masquerade now. But as I am to tell you of the time when I loved to wear this waistcoat, I want to picture to myself those days too in every way. Come! Even the place where we so often used to rest from our hunting and our walks is to contribute to this.'

They walked, and on the way Theresa said to her companion: 'It isn't fair that you let me do all the talking; you already know enough about me, and as yet I don't know the slightest thing about you; so tell me something about yourself in order that I shall have the courage to present to you my story and circumstances as well.' 'Unfortunately,' Wilhelm replied, 'I have nothing to relate except a succession of mistakes and aberrations, and I don't know from whom rather than yourself I would prefer to conceal the confusions in which I have found myself, and am, still enmeshed. Your glance and everything surrounding you, your whole character and your bearing show me that you can be pleased with your past life, that you have moved in a safe sequence of events along a beautiful and straight path, that you have lost no time, and that you have no need to reproach yourself.'

Theresa smiled and rejoined: 'We shall have to wait and see whether you still think like that, when you hear my story.' They went on, and amid some general topics of conversation Theresa asked him: 'Are you free?'—'I believe so, but I don't want to be.'—'Good!' she said, 'that indicates a complicated romance and shows me that you too have something to tell.'

In talking thus they climbed up the hill and sat down by a large oak which spread its shade far around. 'Here,' said Theresa, 'beneath this German tree I will tell you the story of a German girl; listen to me patiently.

'My father was a prosperous nobleman of this province, a

cheerful, lucid, active, gallant man, an affectionate father, an honest friend, and a first-rate host, and the only fault of his I knew was that he was too indulgent towards a wife who did not know how to appreciate him. Unfortunately I must say that of my own mother! Her character was quite the opposite of his. She was quick, unreliable, and without any liking for her house or for myself, her only child; extravagant but beautiful, intelligent, talented, and the delight of a circle that she could attract round her. It is true, her social group was never a large one, or else did not remain so for long. This circle consisted mostly of men, for no woman felt at ease beside her, and still less could she tolerate the merits of a woman. I resembled my father in appearance and attitudes. Just as a young duck immediately makes for water, so from childhood onwards my element consisted of kitchen, store-room, barns and attics. Domestic order and cleanliness seemed to be my only instinct and aim, even while I was still playing. My father was pleased at this and provided purposeful pursuits in stages for my childish endeavours; in contrast, my mother did not love me, and did not hide it for a moment.

'I grew up, and as the years went by my activity increased and so did my father's love for me. When we were alone we went into the fields, or when I was helping him with the accounts, I could really feel how happy he was. When I looked into his eyes, it was as if I were looking within myself, for it was just the eyes which made me completely like him. But in the presence of my mother he did not keep his courage nor his expression; he apologized gently for me when she reproved me vehemently and unjustly; he took up my cause not as if he were able to protect me but as if he could only make excuses for my good qualities. Thus he did not oppose any of her inclinations either; she began to throw herself into acting with the greatest passion, a theatre was set up, and there was no shortage of men of all ages and figures who would appear with her on the stage, although there was often a shortage of women. Lydia, a pleasant girl who had been brought up with me and who promised to be attractive right from her early childhood, had to take the second female parts, and an old chambermaid to represent the mothers and the aunts, while my mother kept for herself the roles of first lovers, heroines and shepherdesses of all kinds. I can't tell you how ridiculous it seemed to me when people, all of whom I knew really well, had dressed up and were standing on the stage, and wanted to be taken for something different from what they were. I always only saw my mother and Lydia, this Baron and that secretary, whether they now appeared as princes and counts or as peasants, and I couldn't understand how they expected me to believe that they were happy or unhappy, in love or indifferent, mean or generous, since for the most part I was precisely informed to the contrary. For that reason too I seldom remained in the audience; I always trimmed the lamps for them, simply in order to have something to do; I prepared the evening meal and next morning, while they were still sleeping, I had already tidied up their wardrobe, as they usually left their garments heaped on top of each other in the evening.

'My mother seemed fully to approve of this activity, but I could not gain her affection; she despised me, and I still well remember how she repeated bitterly on more than one occasion: "If the mother could be as uncertain as the father, it would indeed be difficult to take this housemaid for my daughter." I did not deny that her behaviour gradually alienated me wholly from her, I regarded her actions as if they were those of a stranger, and as I was in the habit of watching the servants like a hawk— for, by the way, this is the basis of all household management— the relationships of my mother and her circle naturally also came to my notice. It could certainly be observed that she did not look at all men in the same way, I paid attention more closely, and soon noticed that Lydia was a confidante and in this capacity was herself becoming more familiar with a passion which she had so often imagined from her early years onward. I knew about all their meetings, but I kept silent and did not say anything to my father whom I was afraid of distressing; but in the end I was forced to tell him. A lot of things they could not undertake without bribing the servants. The latter started to defy me, to neglect my father's instructions and not to carry out my orders; the confusion resulting from this was intolerable to me; I revealed everything to my father and complained to him.

'He listened to me with composure. "Dear child," he finally said with a smile, "I know everything; be calm, bear it with patience, for it is only for your sake that I put up with it."

'I was not calm, I did not have patience. I reproached my father on the quiet; for I did not believe that he needed to tolerate that sort of thing for any reason; I insisted upon order, and I was determined to take the affair to extreme lengths.

'My mother was wealthy in her own right, but spent more than she was entitled to, and, as I indeed noticed, this led to many a scene of explanation between my parents. For a long time there was no improvement in the situation until my mother's passions themselves brought about a kind of development.

'The first lover had been unfaithful to her in a sensational manner; the house, the neighbourhood, her circumstances had become intolerable to her. She wanted to move to another estate, but it was too lonely for her there; she wanted to go to the city, but there she was not important enough. I don't know all that went on between her and my father; enough, he finally decided to agree to her undertaking a journey to Southern France, which she wanted to do, on conditions that I did not learn about.

'Now we were free and lived as in heaven; indeed, I believe that my father lost nothing, even if he did have to pay a considerable sum for her departure. All unnecessary servants were dismissed, and fortune seemed to favour our arrangements; we had a few very good years, everything went as we wished. But unfortunately this happy position did not last long; completely unexpectedly my father was seized by an apoplectic fit which paralysed his right side and deprived him of the ability to speak properly. People had to guess what it was he wanted, for he never brought out the word that he had in his mind. In consequence I came to dread many occasions in which he expressly wished to be alone with me; he indicated with vehement gestures that everyone should leave, and when we were alone together he was not in a position to find the right word. His impatience became extreme, and his situation saddened my innermost being. So much seemed certain to me, that he had something to confide to me that concerned me particularly. How much I desired to find out what it was! Usually I could tell from his eyes whatever it was that he wanted; but now this was in vain! Even his eyes no longer spoke. Only this much was clear to me: he wanted nothing, he desired nothing, he was only struggling to reveal to me something which I unfortunately did not learn. He had another attack, and soon afterwards he became completely inactive and incapacitated; and a little while later he was dead.

'I don't know what made me think that he had hidden a treasure somewhere which he would rather I had after his death than my mother; while he was still alive I already started searching, but I found nothing; after his death everything was sealed up. I wrote to my mother and offered to remain in the house as manager; she would not allow this, and I had to leave the estate. A reciprocal will was found, according to which she was to have possession and enjoyment of everything and I was to be dependent on her, at least for the duration of her whole life. It was now that I first believed that I could understand what my father was hinting at; I felt sorry for him because he had been so weak as to be unjust to me even after his death. For some of my friends went so far as to maintain that it was almost no better than if he had disinherited me, and they wanted me to contest the will, but I could not decide to do that. I respected my father's memory too much; I trusted destiny, I trusted myself.

'I had always been on good terms with a lady in the neighbourhood who was the owner of large estates; she was pleased to receive me, and it was soon easy for me to take charge of her household. She lived in a very regular way and loved order in all things, and I helped her loyally in the struggle with steward and servants. I am neither mean nor envious, but generallly speaking we women are more intent than even a man on insisting that nothing should be wasted. Any sort of fraud is intolerable to us; we want everyone to enjoy only what he is entitled to.

'Now I was in my element again, and I quietly mourned my father's death. My patroness was pleased with me; only one small thing disturbed my calm. Lydia came back; my mother had been so cruel as to cast off the poor girl after she had been thoroughly spoilt and misled. She had learnt in my mother's circle to regard passions as destiny; she was not accustomed to restraining herself in anything. When she unexpectedly appeared again, my benefactress took her in as well; she wanted to give me a helping hand, but was incapable of fitting in.

'At this time the relatives and future heirs of my mistress frequently visited the house and entertained themselves with hunting. Lothario too was often with them; I quite soon noticed how very much he stood out from the others, but I did not relate this to myself in any way. He was polite to everybody, and soon Lydia seemed to be attracting his attention. I was always busy and was seldom with the company; I talked less than usual in his presence: for I won't deny that from earliest times a lively conversation had been the spice of life for me. I had been glad to talk a lot with my father about everything that happened. What we don't discuss, we don't rightly consider. I had never listened more eagerly to anyone than to Lothario when he talked about his travels and campaigns. The world lay clear and open before him, like the area which I had been managing. For instance, I did not hear from him the strange fortunes of an adventurer, nor the exaggerated half-truths of a petty-minded traveller who always put himself into the place of the country which he is promising to depict for us; he did not tell a story but conducted us to the places themselves; I have not often felt such pure pleasure.

'But my satisfaction was inexpressible when I heard him talking about women one evening. The conversation arose quite naturally; some ladies from the neighbourhood had visited us and had been talking in the usual way about the education of women. Our sex was treated unjustly, it was said, the men wanted to reserve all higher culture for themselves, there was an unwillingness to admit us to any scientific studies, and we were required only to be playthings or housekeepers. Lothario said little to all this; but when the group had become smaller, he openly gave his opinion about this subject as well. "It is strange," he exclaimed, "that it is held against a man if he wishes to place a woman at the highest position which she is capable of holding: and what position is higher than the management of the house? If the man wrestles with external conditions, if he has to procure and protect the property, if he even has to take part in government administration, if he is everywhere dependent on circumstances and, I might say, is nowhere in charge, since he has to act expediently when he would like to be rational, be secretive when he would like to be open, and deceptive instead of honest, and if, for the sake of an aim which he never achieves, he has to sacrifice continually his highest ambition, harmony with himself: a good housekeeper is truly in charge within the household and satisfies the needs and desires of an entire family. What is man's greatest happiness if not to carry out what we perceive to be right and proper, and for us to be really masters of the means to our ends? And where should our immediate aims lie, where can they lie, except inside the house? Where do we expect to encounter all indispensable and continually recurring needs, where do we require them to be if not where we get up and lie down, where kitchen, cellar and every kind of provision are always available to us and our dependants? What hard work is needed in order to carry out this constant regime in the daily sequence of events! How few men are in a position where they can return regularly like a star, so to speak, and preside both over day and night! Or design their own domestic implements, plant and reap, save and spend, and always move in their orbit with calm, love and a sense of purpose! Once a woman has gained this inner mastery, then only does she make the man whom she loves into a master; her attentiveness acquires all knowledge, and her enterprise knows how to make use of it all. In this way she is dependent on nobody and procures for her husband true independence, domestic, inward independence; what he owns he sees secured, what he acquires he sees put to good use, and so he can apply his mind to important matters and, if he is lucky, he can be as much service to the state as his wife is at home."

'After this he gave a description of the type of wife he wished for. I blushed, for he was describing my very self. I enjoyed my triumph in secret, all the more as I realized that he had not had me personally in mind, that he did not actually know me. I can recall no pleasanter emotion in my whole life than the fact that a man whom I esteemed so much gave preference not to my person, but to my innermost nature. How rewarded I felt! What encouragement had been given to me!

'When they had gone my worthy friend and patroness said to me with a smile: "What a pity that men often think and say things that they do not allow to be put into practice, else a fine husband for my dear Theresa would have been found straightaway." I joked about her comment and added that, although it was true that men's common sense would look around for housekeepers but that their heart and imagination aspired to other qualities, we housekeepers in fact didn't stand a chance in competition with fascinating and charming girls. I said these words for Lydia's benefit: for she did not conceal that Lothario had made a big impression on her, and at each new visit he seemed to be becoming more attentive to her. She was poor, she was not aristocratic, she could not think of marrying him; but she could not resist the delights of attracting and being attracted. I had never been in love, and was not in love even now; but although I greatly enjoyed seeing how so respected a man judged and defined my own nature, I will nevertheless not deny that I was not completely satisfied by this. I now also wished that he might know me and take a personal interest in me. This wish arose in my mind without any definite thought as to what could follow from it.

'The greatest service which I carried out for my benefactress was my attempt to put in order the fine woodlands on her estates. Unfortunately this delightful property was still run along the old careless lines. There was no trace of planning and order to be found, and there was no end to the stealing and fraud. Many hills were standing desolate, and only the oldest types of tree showed even growth. I went everywhere myself with a skilled forester, I had the woods surveyed, supervised the felling, sowing and planting, and within a short time everything was in motion. I had had male clothing made for me, in order to ride on horseback more easily and also not to be hindered anywhere when I was on foot; I went to a lot of places and was feared everywhere.

'I heard that the group of young friends had again arranged a hunt with Lothario; for the first time in my life I had the idea of *appearing*, or rather in order not to do myself an injustice, of being considered in the eyes of the excellent man to be what I was. I put on my male attire, took the gun over my shoulder and went out with our huntsman in order to wait for the gathering at the boundary. They came, and Lothario did not recognize me immediately; one of the nephews of my benefactress introduced me to him as a skilful forester, made jokes about my youth and continued with his playful approach in my praise for so long that Lothario finally recognized me. The nephew was seconding my intention as if we had arranged it in advance. He gave his account in detail and with appreciation for what I had done for his aunt's estates and therefore also for him.

'Lothario listened attentively, conversed with me, asked about all circumstances concerning the estates and the neighbourhood, and I was pleased to be able to show him what I knew; I passed my test very well, I had laid before him some suggestions for certain improvements so that he might examine them, he approved them, told me about similar examples and confirmed my reasons through the correlation which he gave them. My contentment grew each moment. But unfortunately I wanted only to be known, not to be loved; for—we came home, and I noticed more than usual that the attention which he showed to Lydia seemed to betray a secret liking. I had achieved my aim and was still not calm; from that day onwards he showed me true respect and admirable trust, he habitually talked to me in company, asked my opinion and seemed to have confidence in me, especially in household matters, as if I knew everything. His interest encouraged me greatly; he drew me into the conversation even when the subject was the country's economy and finance, and in his absence I tried to obtain more information about the province, indeed about the whole country. This was easy for me, for there was only repetition on a large scale of what I knew and was personally familiar with on a small scale.

'From this time on he came more frequently to our house. We talked about everything, I may well say, but to a certain extent our conversation always finally turned to matters of an economic nature, even if only in a figurative sense. There was much discussion of the gigantic effects that man can bring about by the consistent application of his energy, his time and his money, and even by means that seem trivial.

'I did not resist the feeling for him which came over me, and I felt, unfortunately all too soon, how intense, cordial, pure and honest my love was, as I believed all the more that his frequent visits were intended for Lydia and not myself. She at least was most emphatically convinced of this; she made me her confidante, and in this way I found myself to some extent consoled. What she interpreted as being so very much to her advantage I found in no way significant; there was no trace of the intention of a serious, permanent union, and I could see all the more clearly the passionate girl's desire to be his at any price.

'This is how things were when the lady of the house surprised me with an unexpected proposal. "Lothario," she said, "offers you his hand and wishes you to spend your life by his side." She expatiated about my qualities and told me what I so gladly heard: that Lothario was convinced that he found in myself the partner whom he had wished for so long.

'I had now attained the height of happiness: a man desired me whom I very much esteemed and in association with whom I saw the prospect of the full, free, extended and useful expression of my inborn tendencies and of the skills I had acquired through practice; the totality of my whole being seemed to have expanded into the infinite. I gave my consent, he came himself, he talked to me alone, he proffered his hand, he looked into my eyes, he embraced me and kissed me on the lips. It was the first and the last such kiss. He confided his whole situation to me, how much his American expedition had cost, what debts he had incurred against his estates, how he had to a certain degree quarrelled with his great uncle about this, and how this worthy man was thinking of providing for him, but in his own way, for sure: he wanted to find him a rich wife, whereas a perceptive man, Lothario maintained, would only be helped by a wife who was a good housekeeper; he was hoping to convince the old man, with his sister's help. He informed me of the situation as far as his means were concerned, of his plans and prospects, and requested my co-operation. It should remain a secret only until his uncle had given his consent.

'He had hardly left before Lydia asked me whether by chance he had said anything about her? I said "no" and bored her with a narrative concerning economic matters. She was restless and moody, and his behaviour when he came back did not improve her condition.

'But I see that the sun will go down shortly! This is your good fortune, my friend, otherwise you would have had to listen to the story, which I so gladly recount to myself, with all its little details. Let me make haste, for we are approaching a period which it is not good to dwell on.

'Lothario introduced me to his excellent sister, and she knew how to present me to the uncle in an appropriate manner; I gained the old man's favour, he agreed with our wishes, and I returned to my benefactress with good news. The matter was no longer a secret in the house; Lydia learned about it, and believed that she was hearing something impossible. When finally she could no longer doubt it, she suddenly disappeared, and we did not know where she had gone off to.

'The day of our union was approaching; I had already often asked him for his portrait, and I reminded him once more of his promise, just as he was about to ride away. "You have forgotten to give me the frame in which you want to have it fitted," he said. This was the case: I had a present from a friend which was very valuable to me. Initials made of her hair had been fixed under the outer glass, inside was the empty ivory on which her picture was to have been painted when she was unfortunately snatched from me by death. Lothario's affection brought me happiness just at the time when her loss was still very painful to me, and I wanted to fill the gap, which she had left with me in her present, by means of my fiancé's picture.

'I hurried to my room, fetched the jewel-case and opened it in his presence; he had scarcely looked in when he caught sight of a medallion with a woman's picture, he took it in his hand, looked at it attentively and asked hastily: "Whose picture is this intended to be?"—"My mother's," I replied.—"But I could have sworn," he exclaimed, "that it was the portrait of a Madame de Saint Alban whom I met in Switzerland a few years ago."—"It is one and the same person," I rejoined, with a smile, "and so, without knowing it, you have met your mother-in-law. Saint Alban is the romantic name my mother uses when she is travelling; she is still in France under that name at present."

'"I am the most wretched of men!" he exclaimed, throwing the picture back into the case; he covered his eyes with his hand and immediately left the room. He flung himself onto his horse; I ran to the balcony and called after him; he turned round and waved to me; he went off in haste—and I've not seen him again.'

The sun went down, Theresa was looking fixedly at its glowing light, and her beautiful eyes filled with tears.

Theresa was silent and placed her hand upon her new friend's hands; he kissed it with sympathy, she dried her tears and stood up. 'Let us go back,' she said, 'and care for our dependants!'

The conversation on the way was not animated; they came in at the garden gate and saw Lydia sitting on a bench; she got up, avoided them and went back into the house; she had a piece of paper in her hand, and two little girls were with her. 'I see that she is still carrying around with her her one consolation, Lothario's letter. Her friend promises her that she shall again live at his side as soon as he feels well; he requests her in the meantime to stay quietly with me. She clings to these words, she consoles herself with these lines, but his friends are in her black books.'

Meanwhile the two children had come up; they greeted Theresa and gave her an account of everything that had happened in the house in her absence. 'You can see here some part of my occupation,' Theresa said. 'I have made an agreement with Lothario's excellent sister; together we are teaching a number of children: I am educating active and obliging housekeepers, and she is taking on those girls who display quieter and more refined gifts; for it is reasonable that men's happiness and the success of the housekeeping should be fostered in every way. When you meet my noble friend, you will begin a new life: her beauty and goodness make her worthy of the adoration of a whole world.' Wilhelm did not venture to say that unfortunately he already knew the beautiful Countess and that his passing contact with her would grieve him eternally; he was very pleased that Theresa did not continue the conversation and that her duties compelled her to return into the house. He was now alone and felt extremely sad to hear the latest news, that the beautiful young Countess likewise felt compelled already to replace the lack of her personal happiness by means of philanthropy; he felt that in her case there was only a need to distract herself and to put the hope of others' happiness in the place of a cheerful enjoyment of life. He called Theresa happy because no changes needed to take place in herself even in the case of that unexpected and sad change. 'How happy above all is he who does not need to throw away his whole previous life in order to unite himself with destiny!' he exclaimed.

Theresa came to his room and begged pardon for disturbing him. 'Here in the wall-cupboard is my whole library,' she said; 'it consists of books that I don't throw away rather than those that I store. Lydia is asking for a religious book; no doubt one or another can be found amongst them. People who are worldly-minded the whole year through take it into their minds that at a time of stress they ought to be devout; they look on everything good and ethical as if it were a medicine which one reluctantly takes when one feels unwell; they see a priest or a moral philosopher only as a doctor whom one can't get out of the house quickly enough; but I gladly admit that my idea of morality is as of a diet which in fact is only a diet if I make it into a rule of conduct and if I don't let it out of my sight throughout the year.'

They looked among the books and found some so-called devotional books. 'Lydia has learned from my mother to have recourse to these books,' said Theresa: 'plays and novels were her staple fare as long as the lover was faithful; his disappearance at once brought these books into favour again. I can't understand at all,' she continued, 'how people have been able to believe that God speaks to us through books and stories. The person to whom the world does not reveal directly what kind of relationship it has with him and whose heart does not tell him what he owes to himself and to others, will surely scarcely learn it from books which are really only sent to give names to our errors.'

She left Wilhelm alone, and he spent his evening inspecting the little library; it had in fact only come together by chance.

For the few days that Wilhelm stayed at her house Theresa always remained herself; she told him at intervals and in great detail the succession of events after the happening affecting her. The day and the hour, the place and the name were present in her memory, and at this point we will sum up briefly what is necessary for our readers to know.

Unfortunately the reason for Lothario's quick disappearance was easy to find: he had met Theresa's mother in the course of their travels, her charms attracted him, she did not withhold her favours from him, and now this unfortunate, transient adventure was removing him from union with a woman whom Nature herself seemed to have fashioned for him. Theresa's attentions remained exclusively within the sphere of her occupation and duties. It was learnt that Lydia was staying secretly in the neighbourhood. She was happy when the marriage did not take place, although the reasons were not known, and it seemed that he complied with her wishes more out of desperation than inclination, more from surprise than reflection, more from boredom than intention.

Theresa kept quiet about this, she made no further claims on Lothario, and even if he had been her husband, she would perhaps have had courage enough to tolerate such a relationship provided it did not disturb her domestic order; at least she often contended that a woman who kept the household together properly could overlook any little whim of her husband and be sure of his return to her at all times.

Theresa's mother had soon brought confusion into the matter of her finances; her daughter had to suffer for it, for she received little from her; the old lady, Theresa's benefactress, died, leaving her the little freehold and a nice capital sum as bequest. Theresa was able immediately to adapt herself to the narrow circumstances, Lothario offered her a better property, and Jarno acted as negotiator: she refused this. 'I want to show on a small scale,' she said, 'that I was worthy of sharing great things with him; but I would like to make the proviso that if chance puts me into an embarrassing position, either on my own account or on behalf of others, I can without hesitation have recourse in the first place to my esteemed friend.'

Nothing remains less concealed and unused than purposeful activity. She had scarcely settled down in her little property when the neighbours already endeavoured to get to know her more closely and to seek her advice, and the new owner of the bordering estates made it clear that it only depended on her to decide whether she would accept his hand and become heir to the largest part of his wealth. She had already mentioned this relationship to Wilhelm and occasionally joked with him about marriages and misalliances.

'There is nothing that causes people to talk more,' she said, 'than when on occasion a marriage takes place which from their point of view they can call a misalliance. And yet misalliances are much commoner than successful marriages; for unfortunately after a short time most unions seem to be in a bad way. The intermarriage of different classes only deserves to be called misalliance in so far as the one partner can have no share in the other's life pattern which has been acquired by birth and custom and has, as it were, become necessary. The different classes have different ways of life which they can't share with one another nor mistake one for the other, and this is why unions of this type are better not contracted; but exceptions are possible, and really happy exceptions too. In this way the marriage of a young girl to an ageing man is always dangerous, and yet I have seen them work really well. From my own point of view I only know one type of misalliance, that is, if I had to entertain and keep up appearances; I would rather give my hand to any honest farmer's son in the neighbourhood.'

Wilhelm now thought of returning and asked his new friend if she would make it possible for him to exchange a few words with Lydia before leaving. The passionate girl allowed herself to be persuaded, he addressed a few friendly words to her, and she rejoined: 'I've got over the first distress; Lothario will be eternally dear to me; but I know what his friends are like, I'm sorry that he's got such people around him. For the sake of a whim the Abbé would be capable of leaving people in the lurch, or indeed of pushing them deliberately into trouble; the doctor would like to have everything settled; Jarno is without feeling, and you are, at all events, without character! You just carry on in this way and let yourself be used as a tool by these three men, they will find plenty more enforcement jobs for you. For a long time—I well know this—they did not like my being about, I had not found out their secret, but I had observed that they were hiding one. Why the locked rooms? Why these strange passages? Why can no one get to the big tower? Why did they banish me to my room, whenever they could? I am willing to admit that it was jealousy that first led me to this discovery, I was afraid that some fortunate rival was hidden away somewhere. Now I don't believe that any more, I am convinced that Lothario loves me and that he wants to be honest with me; but I am just as surely convinced that he is being deceived by his superficial and false friends. If you want to do him a service and if I am to pardon you for the wrong you have done to me, free him from the clutches of these men. But what am I hoping! Deliver this letter to him and repeat its contents: that I shall love him eternally, and that I depend upon his promise. Oh!, she exclaimed, standing up and weeping as she embraced Theresa, 'he is surrounded by my enemies, they will try to persuade him that I have not made any sacrifice on his behalf; oh, the best of men is glad to hear that he is worthy of every sacrifice without being allowed to be grateful for this.'

Wilhelm's parting from Theresa was on a more cheerful note; she hoped to see him again soon. 'You know me completely!' she said, 'you have let me do all the talking; next time it is your duty to reciprocate my frankness.'

On his return journey he had time enough to recall and reflect upon this new, clear-sighted personality. What confidence she had inspired in him! He thought of Mignon and Felix, and of how happy the children could become under her supervision; then he thought of himself and felt what bliss it would be to live close to such a truly humane person. As he approached the castle, the tower and the many passages and side-buildings aroused his attention more than usually; he resolved to take the next opportunity to call Jarno and the Abbé to account about them.

Chapter Seven

When Wilhelm arrived at the castle he found that the splendid Lothario was on the way to complete recovery; the Doctor and the Abbé were not present, only Jarno had remained. Within a short time the convalescent went out riding again, sometimes alone, sometimes with his friends. His discourse was serious and courteous, his conversation instructive and stimulating; traces of a delicate sensitivity were often noticeable, although he tried to hide them, and when this mood showed itself against his will, he almost seemed to disapprove of it.

Thus he was quiet at the table one evening although he looked serene.

'You must surely have had an adventure today,' Jarno finally said, 'and a pleasant one too.'

'What insight you have!' Lothario replied. 'Yes, a very pleasant adventure happened to me. On another occasion I might not perhaps have found it so charming as this time, as it caught me in such a receptive mood. Towards evening I was riding through the villages on the other side of the water, a way which I took often enough in earlier years. My physical indisposition must have made me weaker than I thought; I felt mellow and reborn, as my flagging energies revived. All objects appeared to me in the same light that I had seen them in at earlier times, they were all so delightful, charming and attractive, in a way that they had not appeared to me for a long time. I was in fact aware that this was weakness, but I let myself enjoy it completely, I rode gently on, and it became quite understandable to me how we can grow fond of an illness that puts us in the mood for tender emotions. Perhaps you know what it was that used to take me along this way so often?'

'If I remember aright,' Jarno rejoined, 'it was a trivial love-affair that had developed with the daughter of a farmer.'

'You could call it a serious love-affair,' Lothario countered, 'for we both loved each other, for a fairly long time. Today by chance everything conspired to conjure up the early days of our love in a truly vivid way. The boy again happened to be shaking the cockchafers down from the trees, and the foliage on the ash trees had not progressed further than on the day when I saw them for the first time. I had not seen Margaret for a long time up to now, for she has married someone living far away, only I chanced to hear that she came to visit her father with her children a few weeks ago.'

'So in fact this ride of yours was not such a matter of chance as all that?'

'I don't deny,' Lothario said, 'that I did want to meet her. When I was not far from their home I saw her father sitting by the door; a child of about one year old was standing by him. As I approached, a woman looked quickly out of an upstairs window, and when I came near the door, I heard someone leaping down the stairs. I felt certain that it was she, and I gladly admit that I was flattering myself that she had recognized me and was coming in haste to meet me. But how I was put to shame when she bounded out of the doorway, took hold of the child, whom the horses were approaching, and carried it into the house. It was a disagreeable feeling for me and I was consoled only a little in my vanity when I thought I saw a noticeable reddening of her neck and of the one visible ear, as she hurried away.

'I stopped and spoke to the father, in the meantime glancing covertly at the windows, in case she might be showing herself at one or the other; but I did not see any trace of her. I did not want to ask, and so I rode past. My annoyance was to some extent tempered by surprise: for although I had scarcely seen the face, it none the less hardly seemed changed at all, and after all ten years are quite a time! Indeed, she seemed younger to me, just as slim, just as nimble, her neck if possible even more graceful than previously, while her cheek was equally easily accessible to a delightful blush, at the same time she is the mother of six children, perhaps of even more. This presence fitted in so well with the rest of the enchanted world surrounding me, that I continued riding with an enhanced feeling of rejuvenation and did not turn round at the next stretch of forest until the sun was in the process of setting. Although the falling dew recalled to me the doctor's advice and although it would probably have been more advisable to make straight for home, I nevertheless made my way back again by the side of the farm. I noticed that a female person was walking up and down in the garden, which is surrounded by a small hedge. I rode on the footpath towards the hedge, and found myself not far from the person I was looking for.

'Although the evening sun was in my eyes, I could none the less see that she was busy by the fence which did not conceal her completely. I believed I could recognize my former beloved. As I came up to her, I stood still, not without some stirring of the heart. Some high branches of wild roses, which a gentle breeze was swaying this way and that, prevented me from seeing her figure clearly. I addressed her, asking her how she was. She answered in an undertone: "Very well." Meanwhile I noticed that a child behind the fence was occupied in pulling up flowers, and I took the opportunity to ask where the rest of her children might be? "This is not my child," she said, "that would be starting early!", and at that moment it happened that I could see her face clearly through the branches, and I did not know how I should react to the person I saw. It was my beloved, and it was not. Almost younger and more beautiful than when I had known her ten years ago. "Aren't you the farmer's daughter then?" I asked, half confusedly. "No," she said, "I am her cousin."

'"But you are so very much like each other," I replied.

'"That's what everybody says who knew her ten years ago."

'I continued to ask her this and that; I was enjoying my mistake, although I had already realized it. I could not tear myself away from the living picture of earlier happiness that was standing in front of me. Meanwhile the child had separated herself from her and had gone to the pond to look for flowers. She took her leave and hurried after the child.

'In the meantime I did learn after all that my former beloved was still really in her father's house, and as I was riding, I was occupied with speculations as to whether she herself or the cousin had brought the child to safety from the horses. I turned over the whole story in my mind several times, and I can hardly think of anything that would have had a pleasanter effect on me. But I can feel that I am still ill, and we will ask the doctor if he will release us from what is left over of this mood.'

It tends to be the same with confidences about happy love affairs as with ghost stories: once one has been told, the others flow along to join it of their own accord.

Our little company found much material of this kind in the recollection of past times. Lothario had most to tell. Jarno's stories all had a character of their own, and we already know what Wilhelm had to confess. However, he was fearful that someone might remind him of the story involving the Countess; but nobody thought of this even in the remotest way.

'It is true,' Lothario said, 'there can be no pleasanter emotion in the world than when the heart once again after an interval of indifference responds with love towards a new object, and yet I would gladly have dispensed with this happiness for the length of my life, if fate had been willing to unite me with Theresa. One isn't a young man for ever, and one should not always be a child. What can be more welcome to a man who knows the world and who knows what he has to do in it and to hope from it, than to find a wife who will everywhere be active with him and know how to prepare everything for him, who busies herself with matters which he has to leave on one side, and whose preoccupations spread in all directions while his own may only proceed along a straight path. What a heaven had I dreamt of for myself with Theresa! Not the heaven of a fanciful happiness, but that of a secure life on earth: order in happiness, courage in unhappiness, care for the smallest things, and a soul capable of grasping what is greatest and then letting it go again. Oh, in her I saw indeed the potentialities whose development we admire when we see in history women who appear to us as much more excellent than all men: this clear view of the circumstances, this skill in all instances, this security in the particular by means of which the whole is always in such good condition, without their ever seeming to think of it. You can surely pardon me,' he continued, as he turned towards Wilhelm with a smile, 'if Theresa abducted me from Aurelia; with the former I could hope for a cheerful life, while in the case of the latter there was no thinking even of a happy hour.'

'I don't deny that I came here with much bitterness of heart against you,' Wilhelm replied, 'and that I had intended to criticize severely your behaviour to Aurelia.'

'It deserved blame too,' Lothario said, 'I ought not to have confused my friendship for her with the feeling of love, I ought not to have allowed, in place of the respect which she deserved, an inclination to intrude which she could neither arouse nor sustain. Alas! She was not lovable when she loved, and that is the greatest misfortune which can befall a woman.'

'Let it be,' Wilhelm replied, 'we can't always avoid what is blameworthy, nor that our opinions and actions are deflected in a strange way from their natural and true course; but there are certain duties that we should never lose sight of. May the ashes of our friend rest peacefully! Let us, without reproaching ourselves or blaming her, scatter flowers in pity upon her grave. But at the grave in which the unhappy mother is resting, let me ask you why you don't take charge of the child, of a son whom anyone would be pleased about and whom you seem to be neglecting completely? How can you, with your pure and delicate feelings, utterly deny a father's heart? During all this time you have not as yet mentioned with a single syllable the precious creature about whose charm so much could be related.'

'Who are you talking about?' Lothario put in, 'I don't understand you.'

'About who else but your son, Aurelia's son, the handsome child who lacks nothing for his happiness except the care of an affectionate father!'

'You are mistaken, my friend,' Lothario cried: 'Aurelia did not have a son, least of all by me, I don't know of any child, otherwise I should be happy to accept responsibility for him; but even in the present instance I shall be glad to consider the little fellow as a bequest of hers and to look after his education. Did she indicate in any way that the boy was hers or mine?'

'I don't recall having had a specific indication from her, it was just taken for granted, and I didn't doubt it for a moment.'

'I can give some information here,' Jarno interposed. 'An old woman, whom you must have often seen, brought the child to Aurelia, she received him with passionate warmth and hoped to ease her own sufferings by his presence; what is more, he did provide her with many a pleasurable moment.'

This revelation made Wilhelm very agitated, he thought very much of the good Mignon as well as handsome Felix, and he expressed the wish to extract both children from the position they were in.

'We will soon deal with that,' Lothario replied. 'We can give the extraordinary girl to Theresa, she can't fall into better hands, and as for the boy, I should think you could look after him yourself; for those things which even women are unable to teach us will be learned by children, when we spend time on them.'

'Actually,' Jarno added, 'I think that you ought to give up the stage, for which you really haven't any talent.'

Wilhelm was taken aback; he had to take hold of himself, for Jarno's harsh words had wounded his self-esteem not a little. 'If you can convince me of that,' he rejoined with a forced smile, 'you will do me a service, even though it is only a sad service when someone rouses us from a favourite dream.'

'Without saying anything further about it,' Jarno went on, 'I should like to urge you first to fetch the children; the rest will sort itself out.'

'I am prepared to do this,' Wilhelm rejoined; 'I am disturbed and curious to see if I cannot find out anything further about the boy's destiny; I should like very much to see the girl again who has attached herself to me in a way peculiar to herself.'

It was agreed that he should set off soon.

Next day he had made his preparations, the horse had been saddled, and he only wanted to take leave of Lothario. When the mealtime came, they sat down at the table without waiting for the head of the house; he did not come till late, and then joined them.

'I should like to bet,' said Jarno, 'that today you have again been putting your fond heart to the test, and that you have not been able to resist the desire of seeing your former beloved once more.'

'You've guessed aright!' Lothario replied.

'Let's hear how things went,' Jarno said, 'I am most curious.'

'I don't deny that the adventure was preoccupying my emotions more than was reasonable,' Lothario rejoined; 'I therefore made up my mind to ride over once more and to see in reality the person whose rejuvenated picture had presented me with such a pleasant illusion. I dismounted some distance from the house and had the horses led aside, in order not to disturb the children who were playing in front of the gate. I went into the house, and she came towards me, as chance would have it, for it was she herself, and I recognized her again in spite of the great change. She had become more solidly built and seemed to be taller; her charm showed itself by a sedate disposition, and her cheerfulness had changed into quiet thoughtfulness. Her head, which she had formerly held in so easy and free a manner, was a little bent forward, and her brow was faintly lined.

'She lowered her eyes when she saw me, but no blush gave indication of an inner motion of the heart. I offered her my hand and she gave me hers; I asked after her husband, he wasn't there, I asked after her children, she went to the door and called them, they all came and gathered round her. There is nothing more delightful than to see a mother with a child on her arm, and nothing more worthy of respect than a mother among a lot of children. I inquired about the little ones' names, just in order to have something to say; she asked me to step inside and wait for her father. I accepted the invitation; she led me into the dining-room where I found nearly everything in its old place, and—it was strange, the beautiful cousin, her image, was sitting on the very same stool behind the distaff, where I had so often found my beloved in that very same position. A little girl who resembled her mother exactly had followed us, and so I was standing there in a most strange present time between past and future, as in an orange grove where within a small area blossom and fruit live in stages side by side. The cousin went out to fetch some refreshments, I shook the hand of the one whom I had at one time loved so much and said to her: "I am really happy to see you again."—"It is very good of you to say that to me," she replied; "but I too can assure you that I am inexpressibly happy. How often have I wished only to see you once more in my life! This has been my wish in moments which I thought might be my last." She said this in a calm voice, without emotion, and with that naturalness which formerly caused me such delight in her. The cousin came back, and her father came as well—and I can leave it to you to imagine with what feeling I stayed, and with what feeling I left.'

Chapter Eight

On his way to the city Wilhelm thought about the fine women he knew and about whom he had heard; he was sadly conscious of their strange destinies which recorded little that was cheering. 'Oh, poor Mariane!' he exclaimed, 'what have I still to learn about you? And you, wonderful Amazon, noble protective spirit to whom I owe so much, whom I hope to encounter everywhere and whom unfortunately I find nowhere, in what sad circumstances shall I perhaps find you when we meet again some time!'

In the city no one he knew was at home; he hurried to the theatre, thinking that he would find them rehearsing; everything was quiet, the building seemed empty, but he saw a shutter open. When he came to the stage he found Aurelia's old servant busy sewing together canvas for a new piece of scenery; there was only as much light coming in as was necessary to make her work possible. Felix and Mignon were sitting on the ground near her; both were holding a book, and as Mignon read aloud, Felix repeated all the words after her, as if he knew the letters and knew how to read as well.

The children leapt up and greeted the new arrival, he embraced them most tenderly and led them closer to the old woman. 'Was it you,' he said to her in a serious tone, 'who brought this child to Aurelia?' She looked up from her work and turned her face towards him; he saw her in the full light and stepped back a few paces; it was old Barbara.

'Where is Mariane?' he cried out.—'Far from here,' the old woman replied.

'And Felix? . . .'

'Is the son of this unhappy girl who loved only too tenderly. May you never feel how much you have cost us, and may the treasure that I am handing to you make you as happy as he has made us unhappy!'

She got up to move away; Wilhelm caught hold of her. 'I am not thinking of running away from you,' she said, 'let me go and fetch a document that will give you both pleasure and distress.' She went off, and Wilhelm looked at the boy with a fearful joy; he was not as yet entitled to call the child his son. 'He is yours,' cried Mignon, 'he is yours,' and she pressed the child against Wilhelm's knees.

The old woman came and handed him a letter. 'Here are Mariane's last words,' she said.

'She's dead!' he cried out.

'Yes, dead!' the old woman said; 'I wish I could spare you from all reproaches.'

Wilhelm opened the letter in surprise and confusion; but he had hardly read the opening words when he was seized by bitter grief; he dropped the letter, collapsed on to a grassy bank and stayed lying there for a time. Mignon busied herself with him. In the meantime Felix had picked up the letter and pestered his playmate until she gave way, kneeled down by him and read it aloud to him. Felix repeated the words, and Wilhelm was compelled to hear them twice over. 'If this note ever reaches you, be sorry for your unfortunate beloved, your love brought her death. The boy whose birth I am surviving for only a few days is yours; I die faithful to you, however much appearances may be against me; with you I lost everything that bound me to life. I die contented, since I am assured that the child is healthy and will live. Listen to old Barbara, pardon her, fare well and do not forget me.'

What a painful letter, and one which was yet consoling to him in its enigmatic nature and whose contents did not become truly meaningful to him until the children recited and repeated them in hesitating and stammering tones!

'Now you know!' the old woman exclaimed, without waiting for him to recover; 'thank heaven that after the loss of such a good girl you are left with such a fine child. Nothing will equal your grief when you hear how the good girl remained faithful to you to the end, how unhappy she became, and how she sacrificed everything for you.'

'Let me drink at one and the same time the cup of sorrow and of joy!' Wilhelm called out. 'Convince me, or just persuade me, that she was a good girl, that she deserved my respect as well as my love, and then leave me to my grief at her irreplaceable loss!'

'This is not the time now,' the old woman replied, 'I have things to do and do not wish that we should be found together. Keep it a secret that Felix belongs to you; there would be too many reproaches from the Society concerning my dissimulation hitherto. Mignon won't betray us, she's good and discreet.'

'I've known it a long time and not said anything,' Mignon put in.—'How is that possible?' the old woman cried. 'Who told you?' Wilhelm interposed.

'The Ghost told me.'

'How? Where?'

'In the vault, when the old man drew his knife, I heard the words: 'Call his father!' and then I thought of you.'

'Who was it who called then?'

'I don't know, in my heart, in my head, I was so afraid, I trembled, I prayed, there was a voice, and I understood.'

Wilhelm pressed her to his heart, recommended Felix to her care and went away. It was not until he was about to go that he noticed that she had become much paler and thinner than when he had left her. Of those he knew Madame Melina was the first person he encountered; she greeted him most warmly. 'Oh, I do hope you will find everything with us here as you would like it to be!' she exclaimed.

'I doubt it,' said Wilhelm, 'and don't expect it. Just admit it, all the arrangements have been made with a view to doing without me.'

'Why did you go off then?' his friend rejoined.

'We can't learn soon enough how dispensable we are in the world. What important people we think we are! We think that we alone bring life to the circle in which we move; we imagine that life, nourishment and breath must falter in our absence, and the gap that is caused is scarcely noticed, it is filled so quickly again, indeed it often only becomes the space if not for something better, at least for something more pleasant.'

'And we are not taking into account our friends' sufferings?'

'Our friends too will do well to come to terms with the situation and say: "Do what you can where you are and where you stay, active and obliging and enjoy the present!"'

On further investigation Wilhelm found what he had surmised: opera had been introduced and was absorbing the whole attention of the public. His own parts had in the meantime been filled by Laertes and Horatio, and both attracted much livelier applause from audiences than he had ever been able to procure.

Laertes entered, and Madame Melina called: 'Look at this lucky man who will soon become a capitalist or God knows what!' Wilhelm embraced him and could feel that his coat was made of superior cloth; his other clothing was simple, but all made from good materials.

'Explain the enigma to me.' Wilhelm exclaimed.

'There is still time enough,' Laertes replied, 'to learn that my running hither and thither is now being paid for, that the owner of a big business house is taking advantage of my restlessness, my knowledge and personal connections, and letting me have some part of what he takes; I would give a lot if at the same time I could acquire confidence in women too; for there is a pretty niece in the house and I note that if I wanted to, I could soon be assured of my fortune.'

'Perhaps you haven't yet heard,' said Madame Melina, 'that

in the meantime there has also been a marriage within our circle. Serlo has officially married the beautiful Elmira, as her father was unwilling to approve of their secret intimacy.'

They went on talking in this way about many things that had happened in his absence, and he could not help being aware that really he had been dismissed long ago as far as the spirit and attitude of the company were concerned. He awaited with impatience the old woman's visit which was to take place late in the night. She wished to come when everyone was asleep and demanded precautions similar to those of a young girl about to steal to her lover. Meanwhile he must have read Mariane's letter through a hundred times; with inexpressible delight he read the word 'faithful' in her own hand, and with terror the announcement of her coming death, whose approach she did not seem to fear.

Midnight had passed when there was a rustling at the half-open door and the old woman entered with a little basket. 'I am to tell you the story of our sufferings,' she said, 'and I must expect you to sit there unmoved, and that you are awaiting me so anxiously only in order to satisfy your curiosity, and that now as then you will wrap yourself in your cold self-love, while our heart is breaking. But look here! This is how I brought out the bottle of champagne on that happy evening, put three glasses on the table, and you began to deceive and lull us with pleasant children's tales, just as I must now enlighten you and keep you awake with sad truths.'

Wilhelm did not know what to say when she let the cork fly and filled the three glasses.

'Drink!' she cried after she had quickly emptied her sparkling glass. 'Drink, before the spirit is lost! This third glass is to stay untouched while the spray disappears, in memory of my unhappy friend. How red were her lips when she drank to your health on that occasion! Alas, they are now eternally pale and rigid!'

'You Sibyl! You Fury!' Wilhelm cried out, leaping up and banging his fist on the table, 'what evil spirit possesses and drives you? Who do you think I am, that you should believe that the simplest narrative of Mariane's death and suffering will not hurt me deeply, and that you still need to use such hellish tricks in order to make my martyrdom more complete? If your insatiable gluttony goes so far that you must carouse at the funeral feast, then drink and talk. I always detested you, and I still can't think of Mariane as innocent when I look at you, her companion.'

'Gently, good sir!' the old woman replied. 'You won't disconcert me. You are still very much in our debt, and nobody has to take insults from a debtor. But you are right, even my simplest narrative is punishment enough for you. So hear now about Mariane's struggle and victory, so that she might remain yours.'

'Mine?' exclaimed Wilhelm, 'what sort of fairy-story do you want to embark on now?'

'Don't interrupt,' she interposed, 'listen to me and then you can believe what you like, in any case it's really all the same now. Did you not find and take with you a note on the last evening that you came to us?'

'I didn't find the note until I had gone; it was entangled in the scarf which I picked up and took away because of my ardent love.'

'What did the paper contain?'

'The expectations of a peeved lover that he would be better received in the night to come than he had been yesterday. And I saw with my own eyes that the promise made to him was kept, for he slunk away from your house shortly before daybreak.'

'You may well have seen him; but it is only now that you will learn what happened under our roof, how sadly Mariane spent that night, and with what vexation I spent it. I will be completely honest, without denying or explaining away the fact that I was trying to persuade Mariane to accept the advances of a certain Norberg; it was with reluctance that she agreed, indeed I might say, obeyed me. He was rich, he seemed to be in love, and I hoped that he would be constant. Immediately after this he had to go on a journey, and Mariane met you. The things I had to put up with, to prevent, and to tolerate! "Oh!" she exclaimed a number of times, "if only you had spared my youth and innocence a further four weeks, I would have found a worthy object of my love, I would have been worthy of him, and love would have been allowed to give with a tranquil mind what I have now sold against my will." She yielded completely to her inclination, and it's not for me to ask if you were happy. I had unlimited control of her reason, for I knew all the ways of satisfying her little fancies; I had no power over her heart, for she never sanctioned what I did for her or what I impelled her to do if her heart was not in agreement; she yielded only to unconquerable need, and the extremity soon seemed very oppressive to her. During the early days of her childhood she had lacked nothing; her family lost their fortune due to a confused series of circumstances, the poor girl had been used to all kinds of necessities of life, and her little mind had been impressed with certain good principles which made her uncomfortable without helping her much. She hadn't the slightest aptitude for worldly matters, she was innocent in the true sense; she had no idea that it was possible to buy without paying; she was afraid of nothing more than being in debt; she would always have preferred to give rather than to take, and it is only such a position that would make it possible to compel her to yield herself in order to get rid of a collection of small debts.'

'And couldn't you have rescued her?' Wilhelm cried.

'Oh, yes,' the old woman rejoined, 'with hunger and distress, with worry and privation, and I was never prepared for that.'

'You revolting and base procuress! So you made a sacrifice of the unfortunate girl? So you surrendered her to your thirst and your voracious appetite?'

'You would do better to moderate yourself and to stop being abusive,' the old woman replied. 'If you want to curse, go into your big, elegant houses where you will find mothers who are really anxious to find the most revolting husband for a sweet and lovely girl, provided that the man is wealthy enough. See how the poor creature trembles and quivers at her fate and finds consolation nowhere until some experienced woman friend makes it comprehensible to her that the married state gives her the right to dispose of her heart and her person as she pleases.'

'Be quiet!' cried Wilhelm; 'do you believe, then, that one crime can be excused by another? Tell your story without making further comments!'

'And listen without blaming me! Mariane became yours against my will. I have nothing to reproach myself in this affair at least. Norberg came back, he hurried to see Mariane who received him coldly and peevishly and did not allow him to kiss her. I needed all my ingenuity in order to excuse her behaviour; I indicated to him that a father confessor had appealed to her conscience, and that a conscience had to be respected as long as it was vocal. I got him to leave and promised to do my best. He was rich and vulgar, but he had a basic kindliness and loved Mariane very much. He promised me he would be patient, and I made all the more efforts not to put him too much to the test. I had a hard task with Mariane; I persuaded her, indeed I can say that in the end I compelled her, with the threat that I would leave her, to write to her lover and invite him at night-time. *You* came and snatched up his reply by chance in the scarf. Your unexpected presence had played a nasty trick on me. You had scarcely gone before the torture began afresh; she swore that she could not be unfaithful to you and was so passionate and beside herself that she wrung heartfelt pity from me. In the end I promised her that for this night too I would calm Norberg down and get him away on all sorts of pretexts; I begged her to go to bed, only she didn't seem to trust me; she remained dressed and finally went to sleep in her clothes, agitated and tearful as she was.

'Norberg came; I tried to put him off, I painted for him her pangs of conscience and her remorse in the blackest colours; he wanted only to see her, and I went into the room to prepare her; he came after me, and we both moved to her bedside at the same time. She awoke, started up angrily and tore herself from our arms; she entreated and begged, she implored, threatened and gave assurance that she would not yield. She was careless enough to let fall a few words about her true passion, which poor Norberg was compelled to interpret in a religious sense. At last he left her, and she shut herself in. I kept him with me for quite a time further and talked to him about her condition, saying that she was pregnant and that the poor girl must be treated with consideration. He felt so proud at being about to be a father and was looking forward so much to a boy that he agreed to everything that she demanded of him and promised that he would spend some time away from her rather than cause his beloved anxiety and harm her with his emotions. With these thoughts he crept away from me in the morning, and if you were standing sentry, sir, nothing more would have been needed to ensure your happiness than to look into the heart of your rival whom you thought to be so favoured and fortunate and whose appearance plunged you into despair.'

'Are you telling the truth?' Wilhelm said.

'So much so,' said the old woman, 'that I am still hoping to make you desperate.

'Yes, indeed, you would certainly despair if I could paint for you the picture of the following morning as it really was. How cheerful she was on waking up! In what friendly tones did she summon me in! How warmly she thanked me! How sincerely she pressed me to her heart! "Now I can again take pleasure in myself and my personal appearance", she said, as she stepped smiling in front of the mirror, "since I belong once more to myself and to the one friend I have loved. How delightful it is to have won! What a heavenly feeling it is, to follow one's heart! How grateful I am to you for taking care of me and for employing your wit and sense to my advantage for once! Stay with me and consider what it is that can make me completely happy!"

'I gave way to her, I did not want to provoke her, I flattered her expectations, and she caressed me most charmingly. If she left the window for a moment, I had to stand guard and, once and for all, it was *you* who were expected to go past. She wanted to see you at least; in this restless way the whole day was passed. We expected you to come at the usual time that night. I was on the look-out by the stairs, the time dragged, and I went in to her again. To my surprise I found her wearing her officer's costume; she looked incredibly happy and attractive. "Don't I deserve to appear in a man's clothing today? Didn't I behave bravely? My lover shall see me today as on the first occasion, I want to press him to my heart as fondly as at that time, and more freely; for am I not now much more his than I was then, since a noble resolve had not as yet made me free? But," she added after some thought, "I still haven't entirely won, I've still got to take the boldest step to be worthy of him and to be sure of his possession; I must reveal everything to him, disclose my whole position to him and then leave it to him to choose whether he will keep me or cast me off. I am preparing this scene for him, and for myself; and if his heart were capable of rejecting me, I would then belong to myself entirely again; I would find my consolation in my punishment and suffer everything that fate might wish to inflict upon me."

'It was with these views and expectations, sir, that the dear girl was awaiting you; you did not come. Oh! How am I to describe the condition of waiting and hoping? I can still see you before me, Mariane; with what love and fervour you were speaking of the man whose cruelty you had not yet experienced!'

'Dear, good Barbara,' cried Wilhelm, jumping up and taking the old woman by the hand, 'we have now had enough pretence and preparation! Your unconcerned, calm and satisfied tone of voice has betrayed you. Give Mariane back to me! She is alive, she is nearby. It is not for nothing that you have chosen this late and lonely hour for your visit, it is not for nothing that you have been preparing me with this delightful story. Where is she? Where are you hiding her? I will believe anything you like, I promise to do so, if you will show her to me and give her back into my arms again! I wish to go on my knees before her, to beg her forgiveness, to congratulate her on her struggle and on her victory over herself and you, and to lead my Felix to her. Come! Where are you keeping her hidden? Don't leave *her*, don't leave me in uncertainty any longer. You've achieved your purpose. Where have you concealed her? Come! Let me reveal her with this light, let me see her lovely face again!'

He had raised the old woman from her chair, she looked at him intently, tears fell from her eyes, and a great grief took hold of her. 'What unhappy error is allowing you still to hope for one moment?' she cried out. 'Yes, certainly, I have hidden her, but under the ground; neither the light of the sun nor the intimacy of a candle will ever again shine upon her lovely face. Take dear little Felix to her grave and tell him that's where your mother lies, whom your father condemned without a hearing. Her dear heart is no longer beating impatiently in the hope of seeing you, she is not waiting in some neighbouring room for the end of my story or fairy-story; she has been received in that dark chamber where no betrothed can follow and which she cannot leave to meet a lover.'

She collapsed on to the ground by a chair and wept bitterly; Wilhelm was for the first time convinced that Mariane was dead; he was in a sorrowful state of mind. The old woman raised herself up. 'I've nothing further to say to you,' she cried, and threw a package on to the table. 'These letters here may put your cruelty completely to shame; read these pages with dry eyes if you can.' She crept quietly away, and Wilhelm did not have the heart to open the letter-case that night, he had given it to Mariane himself, he knew that she used meticulously to keep in it every note she had received from him. Next morning he steeled himself; he untied the ribbon, and little notes written in pencil in his own hand fell towards him and recalled to him every situation from the first day of their delightful association up to the last day of their cruel separation. But not without the most acute distress did he read through a little collection of notes which had been written to him and which, as he saw from the contents, had been sent back by Werner.

'None of my letters has been delivered to you; my beseeching and imploring has not reached you; did you give these cruel orders yourself? Am I never to see you again? Once more I make the attempt, and I beg you: come, oh come! I don't ask to keep you, if I can only press you to my heart once more.'

'When I used to sit with you, holding your hands, looking into your eyes, and when I said to you with my heart full of love and trust: "Dear, dear, good man and husband!", you liked to hear this so much, I had to repeat it so often to you, I repeat it once again: dear, dear, good man and husband! Be kind as you used to be, come and do not let me be ruined in my misery!'

'You think I am guilty, I am too, but not in the way you think. Come, so that I may only receive the one consolation of being known completely by yourself, whatever may happen to me afterwards.'

'I implore you to come not only for my sake, but also for your own. I feel the unbearable grief that you are suffering in taking flight from me; come, so that our separation may be less cruel! I was perhaps never worthy of you except at the moment when you are casting me back into unbounded wretchedness.'

'By all that is holy, by all that can move a human heart, I cry unto you! It is a matter of a soul, of a life, of two lives one of which must be eternally dear to you. Your suspiciousness prevents you from believing this too, and yet I shall pronounce these words at the hour of my death: the child in my womb is yours. Since I have loved you, no other man has as much as pressed my hand; would that your love and your integrity had been my companions in earlier times!'

'You don't wish to hear me? So in the end I suppose I shall have to be silent, but these papers shall not disappear, perhaps they can still talk to you when my lips are covered by a shroud and the voice of your remorse can no longer reach my ears. My only consolation, throughout my sad life to its final moment, will be that I was without guilt in my behaviour towards you, even if I might not call myself innocent.'

Wilhelm could not read further; he gave way completely to his grief, but he was even more afflicted when Laertes came in, from whom he tried to conceal his emotions. The latter brought out a purse containing ducats which he counted and reckoned, assuring Wilhelm that there was nothing better in the world than being in the way to becoming rich; and that in this case there was nothing that could interrupt us or hold us back. Wilhelm remembered his dream and smiled; but at the same time he also recalled with a shudder that Mariane had deserted him in that dream vision in order to follow his dead father, and that finally both had hovered around the garden like ghosts.

Laertes dragged him away from his meditation and took him to a café where he was at once surrounded by a number of people who at one time had been glad to see him on the stage; they were pleased to see him, but regretted that, as they had heard, he was thinking of giving up the stage; they spoke in such positive and sensible terms about him and his activity, about the extent of his talent and about their hopes that finally Wilhelm exclaimed, not without feeling: 'Oh, how infinitely valuable this sympathestic understanding would have been a few months ago! How instructive and encouraging! I should never have turned my mind so definitely from the stage, and I should never have got to the point of despairing of the audience.'

'There should be no need of that at all,' an oldish man said, stepping forward; 'the audiences are large, while reason and true feeling are not so rare as people believe; only the artist must never expect unreserved acclaim for what he produces: for it is the unreserved applause which is of least worth, and the gentlemen don't like the sort of applause which is qualified. I know very well that in life as in art we have to ask ourselves if we want to do anything and be productive; but when the work has been completed, we may listen attentively to many people, and from these many voices we are able with some practice to form complete judgement; for those who could save us the trouble keep quiet enough for the most part.'

'That's just what they shouldn't do!' said Wilhelm. 'I have so often heard it said that people who themselves kept silent, even about admirable works, none the less complained and regretted that there is this silence.'

'So let us make ourselves heard today,' a young man exclaimed, 'you must dine with us, and we will make up for everything that we have continued to owe to you and often to the good Aurelia.'

Wilhelm declined the invitation and went to Madame Melina whom he wanted to talk to about the children, since he was thinking of taking them away from her.

Wilhelm was not the best person to keep the old woman's secret. He gave himself away on seeing the handsome Felix again. 'Oh my child!' he exclaimed, 'my dear child!' He lifted him up and pressed him to his heart. 'Father, what have you brought for me?' the child said. Mignon looked at them both as if she wanted to warn them not to betray themselves.

'What's this new development?' said Madame Melina. They attempted to take the children out of the way, and Wilhelm who did not believe that he had to keep the old woman's secret in strictest confidence revealed the whole relationship to his friend. Madame Melina looked at him with a smile. 'Oh! These credulous men!' she exclaimed; 'so long as something is under their eyes, it is very easy to impose it upon them; but to make up for this, on other occasions they refuse to look to their right or left and value only what they previously imprinted with the stamp of wilful passion.' She could not suppress a sigh, and if Wilhelm had not been quite blind, he could not have avoided noticing from her behaviour a fondness for him that had never been wholly overcome.

He then talked to her about the children, how he was thinking of keeping Felix with him and sending Mignon to the country. Although Madame Melina was sorry to be separated from both children at the same time, she thought that the proposal was a good one, indeed a necessary one. Felix was running wild while in her care, and Mignon seemed to need fresh air and different conditions; the dear child was poorly and unable to recover.

'Don't be led astray,' Madame Melina continued, 'because I expressed some doubts as to whether the boy really does belong to you. The old woman is not to be trusted much, it is true, but someone who thinks out a falsehood to serve to his advantage is also capable of telling the truth once in a way, if the truth seems useful to him. The old woman had deluded Aurelia into thinking that Felix was a son of Lothario, and we women have the ability of having a true affection for the children of our lovers, even if we don't know the mother or if we cordially hate her.' Felix came bounding in, and she embraced him with a vivacity that was unlike her normal self.

Wilhelm hurried home and asked for the old woman, but she would not promise to come to see him except at dusk; he greeted her peevishly and said to her: 'There is nothing more shameful in the world than to make use of lies and fairy-tales! You've already done a lot of harm in this way, and now, when your word could decide about my life's happiness, I am full of doubts and dare not take in my arms the child, whose carefree possession would make me exceedingly happy.'

'If I am to be honest,' the old woman replied, 'your behaviour seems to me to be quite unbearable. And even if he were not your son, he is the most lovely and pleasant child in the world, someone you would be glad to buy at any price, just to have him around all the time. Isn't it worth it for you to take an interest in him? Don't I deserve a small allowance for my future in return for the way I've looked after him? Oh, you gentlemen who want for nothing, it's all very well for you to talk about truth and honesty; but the way a poor creature who receives no assistance for her meagre needs and who has no friend, no advice and no help to turn to in her difficulties, the way she has to make her way through selfish people and be in want on the quiet—there would be quite a bit to be said about that if you were willing and able to listen. Have you read Mariane's letters? They are the ones she wrote during that unhappy time. It was in vain that I tried to approach you and get these notes to you; your cruel brother-in-law had made you so inaccessible that all cunning and guile were useless, and finally, when he threatened me and Mariane with prison, I just had to give up all hope. Doesn't it all fit in with what I have said? And doesn't Norberg's letter confirm the whole story beyond all doubts?'

'What letter?' asked Wilhelm.

'Didn't you find it in the letter-case?' asked the old woman.

'I haven't read everything yet.'

'Just give me the letter-case! Everything hinges on this document. Norberg's unfortunate note caused the sad confusion, another one of his may untie the knot, in so far as the thread is still of any importance.' She took a sheet of paper from the letter-case, Wilhelm recognized that hated handwriting, he pulled himself together and read:

'Just tell me, girl, what gives you such power over me? For I would not have thought that a goddess herself could change me into a sighing lover. Instead of hurrying to me with open arms, you draw back; indeed the way you behaved could have been taken for revulsion. Is it right that I had to spend the night with old Barbara sitting on a trunk in a small room? And my beloved was only two doors away. It's mad, I'm telling you! I have promised to give you time to think matters over and not to put pressure on you straightaway, and each lost quarter of an hour is enough to drive me mad. Have I not given you presents, as best I knew how and was able to? Do you still doubt my love? What do you want? Tell me! You shall lack nothing. I could wish that the priest who filled your head with such rubbish should become dumb and blind. Why did you have to go to that sort of priest! There are so many who are lenient with young people to some extent. Enough, I tell you, things will have to change, I must have an answer in a few days; for I am going away again soon, and if you are not going to be friendly and agreeable once more, you won't see me again . . .'

The letter continued in this vein for a considerable length, kept returning to the same point, to Wilhelm's painful satisfaction, and testified to the truth of the story he had heard from Barbara. A second letter proved clearly that Mariane had not given way later either, and from these and a number of other papers Wilhelm learned, not without deep grief, the unhappy girl's story up to the hour of her death.

The old woman had gradually brought the crude fellow to book by telling him about Mariane's death and leading him to the belief that Felix was his son; he had sent her money several times, but she had kept it for herself, as she had talked Aurelia into taking responsibility for the child's upbringing. But unfortunately these secret earnings did not last long. Norberg had consumed the greater part of his fortune in riotous living, and had hardened his heart against his first presumed son with a series of love-affairs.

However plausible all this sounded and however well it all fitted together, none the less Wilhelm did not as yet trust himself to giving way to feelings of joy; he appeared to be afraid of a gift presented to him by an evil spirit.

'Time alone can heal your sceptisim,' said the old woman, guessing his state of mind. 'Look on the child as a strange one, and pay attention to him all the more closely, take note of his gifts, his nature, his talents, and if you do not gradually recognize yourself in him, you must have bad eyesight. For I can assure you, if I were a man, nobody would foist a child on to me; but it is a good thing for women that men are not so keen-sighted in these cases.'

After all this Wilhelm came to an understanding with the old woman; he agreed to take Felix with him, she was to take Mignon to Theresa and after that to live wherever she wanted on a small pension which he promised her.

He had Mignon sent for in order to prepare her for this change. —'Master,' she said, 'keep me with you! It will be good for me as well as hurting me.'

He put it to her that she had been growing up recently and that after all something would have to be done for her further education.—'I am sufficiently educated,' she replied, 'to love and to mourn.'

He drew her attention to her health, saying that she needed continuous care and the guidance of a clever doctor.—'Why should people care for me,' she said, 'when there is so much that needs caring for?'

After he had made great efforts to convince her that he could not take her with him now and that he wished to take her to people at whose house he would often see her, she appeared not to have heard anything at all about these arrangements. 'You don't want me with you?' she said. 'Perhaps it is better if you send me to the old Harpist! The poor man is so alone.'

Wilhelm tried to make her understand that the old man was well looked after.—'I long to be with him every hour,' the child replied.

'But I didn't notice,' said Wilhelm, 'that you were so fond of him when he was still living with us.'

'I was afraid of him when he was awake; it was just his eyes that I could not look at; but when he was sleeping, I was glad to sit down by him, I kept the flies off him and did not tire of gazing upon him. Oh, he has helped me in terrible moments, nobody knows how much I owe him. If I had only known the way, I would have run off to him before now.'

Wilhelm explained the position to her at length and said that she was a sensible child, and so this time too she should follow his wishes.—'Reason is cruel,' she rejoined, 'the heart is better. I will go wherever you like, but leave me your Felix!'

After a lot of discussion this way and that she persisted in keeping to her own view, and in the end Wilhelm had to decide to hand over both children to the old woman and to send them to Miss Theresa. This became all the easier for him as he was still afraid of accepting the handsome Felix as his son. He would take him in his arms and carry him around; the child liked to be lifted up in front of the mirror, and without admitting it to himself, Wilhelm liked to take him in front of the mirror and there to try to spot resemblances between himself and the child. If the similarity appeared for a moment to be very likely, he pressed the child to his heart, but suddenly, terrified by the thought that he might be deceiving himself, he put the child down and let him run off. 'Oh!' he exclaimed, 'if I were to consider this inestimable treasure to be my own, and it were then snatched from me, I should be the unhappiest of all men!'

The children had left, and Wilhelm now wanted to take leave formally from the theatre, as he felt that he had already departed and needed only to be off. Mariane was no longer alive, his two protective spirits had gone away, and his thoughts were hurrying after them. The lovely boy hovered before his mind's eye like an attractive, uncertain vision, he saw him going through fields and woods with Theresa and being educated in the open air by a frank and cheerful companion; Theresa had become even dearer to him since he began thinking of the child being in her company. Even as a member of an audience at a theatre he recalled her with a smile; he had almost adopted her attitude, stage performances no longer provided him with any sense of illusion.

Serlo and Melina were extremely polite towards him as soon as they noticed that he was making no further claim to his previous position. Some members of the public wanted to see him on the stage again; it would have been impossible for him, and within the theatre company nobody wished it except possibly Madame Melina.

He now bade a final farewell to this friend; he was moved, and said: 'If only man would not presume to promise anything for the future! He is incapable of fulfilling the slightest undertaking, let alone a project of significance. How ashamed I am to think of what I promised you all on that unhappy night when we had been herded together in a miserable inn, robbed, sick, injured and wounded as we were. How misfortune heightened my boldness at that time, and what treasure I thought I had found in my good intentions; now nothing has come of it all, absolutely nothing! I leave you as a debtor, and it is my good fortune that my promise was given no more attention than it deserved, and that nobody has ever admonished me on that account.'

'Don't be unjust to yourself!' Madame Melina replied; 'if nobody else recognizes what you did for us, I certainly shall not fail to appreciate it; for our whole situation would be completely different if we had not had you. It is, after all, the same with our intentions as with our wishes; they no longer look like themselves, when they have been realized and fulfilled, and we believe that we have not done or achieved anything.'

'You won't allay my conscience with your kind interpretation,' Wilhelm answered, 'and I shall always see myself as your debtor.'

'Indeed, it is quite possible that this is what you are,' Madame Melina rejoined, 'only not in the way you think. We consider it shameful not to keep a promise that we have made verbally. Oh my friend, a good person always promises too much simply by his presence! The confidence that he induces, the liking that he calls forth, and the hopes that he kindles are unending; he is a debtor, and remains one, without knowing it. Farewell! Although our external circumstances worked out really well under your guidance, your departure will leave a void within me that cannot be filled again all that easily.'

Before leaving the city Wilhelm wrote another lengthy letter to Werner. It is true, they had exchanged a number of letters, but as they could not agree, they had finally stopped writing. Now Wilhelm had made the approach again; he was about to do what Werner wanted so much, he could say: 'I am leaving the theatre and associating with the men whose acquaintance must lead me in every sense to a pure and stable form of activity'. He inquired about his finances, and it now seemed to him strange that he had not troubled about them for so long. He did not know that it is the nature of all those people who attach much importance to their inner development that they should neglect outward circumstances completely. Wilhelm had found himself in this position; he seemed to notice now for the first time that he needed outward means in order to achieve lasting effects. He went away in a very different mood from the first time; the prospects appearing before him were attractive, and on his way he hoped to experience something agreeable.

Chapter Nine

When he came to Lothario's estate he found much change. Jarno came to meet him with the news that the Uncle had died and Lothario had gone over to take possession of the estate. 'You have come just at the right time,' he said, 'to help me and the Abbé. Lothario has asked us to carry out negotiations for important properties in the neighbourhood; preparations had already been made some time ago, and now we are able to find money and credit just at the right moment. The only problematic aspect of the matter was that a business-house from abroad also had its eye on the same properties; in short, we have now made up our minds to make common cause with the business-house, since otherwise we should have been bidding each other up without any need or sense. It seems that we are dealing with a clever man. At the moment we are making calculations and estimates; we must also consider from the point of view of agricultural economy how we divide up the land so that everyone receives an agreeable property.' The papers were placed before Wilhelm, they showed fields, meadows and castles, and although Jarno and the Abbé seemed to understand the matter very well, Wilhelm nevertheless wished that Miss Theresa might be involved in the discussions.

They spent several days on this work, and Wilhelm had hardly any time to talk about his adventures and his dubious paternity to his friends who treated with indifference and frivolity a matter which was so important to him.

He had noticed that on occasions at table or on walks they suddenly stopped talking in the midst of confidential conversations, that they gave another twist to their words and in this way indicated at least that they had much to deal with among themselves that was concealed from him. He remembered what Lydia had said and found it all the more convincing as a whole side of the castle had always been inaccessible to him. Up to now he had looked in vain for the way of entering certain galleries and in particular the old tower, which he knew quite well from the outside.

One evening Jarno said to him: 'We can now look upon you so completely as one of ourselves that it would be unfair if we did not initiate you more deeply into our secrets. It is right that a man who is making his first appearance in the world has a confident opinion of himself, that he believes he can acquire many advantages for himself, and that he attempts to make everything possible; but when his development has come to a certain stage, it is beneficial if he can learn to lose himself in a sizeable group, to live for the sake of others, and to be forgetful of himself in an activity based on duty. Here for the first time he will come to know himself; for it is really in action that we may be compared with others. You are to learn soon what a small world there is near to you and how well you are known in this small world; be dressed and in readiness early tomorrow morning before dawn.'

Jarno came at the arranged time and led him through known and unknown rooms in the castle, then through some galleries, and they finally arrived at a big old door which was heavily reinforced with iron. Jarno knocked, and the door opened a little so that someone could slip inside. Jarno pushed Wilhelm in without following him. The latter found himself in a dark and narrow enclosure, it was black all around him, and when he tried to take a step forward, he knocked into something. A voice that was not completely unfamiliar called to him, 'Come in!' and now for the first time he noticed that the sides of the space in which he was were only hung with curtains through which a weak light glimmered. 'Come in!' the voice repeated; he lifted up the curtain and went inside.

The room where he now was appeared to have previously been a chapel; instead of an altar there was a large table covered with a green cloth at the top of some steps, and above this it seemed that a closed curtain was concealing a picture; at the sides there were beautifully fashioned bookcases which were sealed off by fine wire grating, as normally seen in libraries, only instead of books he saw many scrolls stacked up. There was nobody in the room; the rising sun shone through the stained glass windows just in Wilhelm's direction and gave him a friendly greeting.

'Do sit down!' a voice called which seemed to be sounding from the altar. Wilhelm sat in a small arm-chair which was placed against the entrance; there was no other seat in the whole room, and he had to be resigned to this one although the morning sunlight dazzled him; the seat was fixed, all he could do was to shade his eyes with his hand.

In the meantime the curtain above the altar opened with a slight noise and revealed a dark, empty aperture within a frame. A man in everyday clothes stepped forward and greeted him, saying: 'Don't you recognize me? As well as the other things which you would like to know, would you not also wish to find out where your grandfather's art collection is at present? Do you no longer remember the picture which attracted you so much? I wonder where the sick prince may be pining now?'—Wilhelm found no difficulty in recognizing the stranger who had conversed with him in the inn on that important evening. 'Perhaps we shall agree sooner this time about fate and character,' the latter went on.

Wilhelm was about to answer when the curtain was quickly closed again. 'Strange!' he said to himself, 'could it be that fortuitous happenings have a connection? And might what we call fate be merely chance? I wonder where my grandfather's collection may be. And why am I reminded of it in these solemn moments?'

He had no time for further thoughts, for the curtain opened again, and a man stood before him whom he at once recognized as the country pastor who had joined him and the merry party on that trip by water; he resembled the Abbé, although he did not seem to be the same person. With a cheerful face and a dignified expression the man started to talk: 'The educator's duty is not to preserve his pupil from error, but to guide him as he goes astray, indeed, to let him swallow his error in full measure. That is wisdom of the teachers. Whoever only has a taste of his error husbands it carefully, he takes pleasure in it as a rare happiness, but he who consumes error to the full must get to know it for what it is, unless he is mad.' The curtain closed again, and Wilhelm had time to think about the matter. 'What error can the man be talking about,' he said to himself, 'if not the one which has dogged me all my life, the fact that I looked for educational development where none was to be found, and that I imagined I could acquire a talent for which I did not have the slightest ability.'

The curtain was opened more quickly, an officer stepped forward and said in passing only the words: 'Get to know the people in whom one may have confidence.' The curtain closed, and Wilhelm did not need to think long before recognizing this officer as the one who had embraced him in the Count's grounds and had been responsible for his assuming that Jarno was a recruiting officer. How this man had come here and who he might be was a complete mystery to Wilhelm.—'If so many people have taken an interest in me, why did they not guide me more strictly and earnestly? Why did they favour my playing, instead of leading me away from it?'

'Don't remonstrate with us!' a voice called; 'you have been saved, and are on the way to the goal. You will not regret any of your follies nor wish for any of them back; no happier fate can befall anyone.' The curtain separated, and the old King of Denmark in full armour was standing in the opening. 'I am your father's ghost,' the figure said, 'and I go away comforted since my wishes for you have been fulfilled more completely than I conceived them even. Steep places can only be climbed by means of détours, in the plains straight paths lead from one place to another. Farewell and remember me when you are enjoying what I have prepared for you!'

Wilhelm was extremely taken aback, he believed he was hearing his father's voice, and yet again it was not his voice; he found himself in the most confused situation because of his present position and his memories.

He did not have long to reflect before the Abbé appeared and placed himself behind the green table. 'Come along here,' he called to his surprised friend. On the table-cloth was a little scroll. 'Here is your certificate of apprenticeship,' the Abbé said, 'consider it well, its contents are important.' Wilhelm took it up, opened it and read:

Certificate of Apprenticeship

'Art is long, life short, judgment difficult, opportunity fleeting. Acting is easy, thinking difficult, acting according to one's thoughts uncomfortable. Every beginning is cheerful, the threshold is the place of expectation. The boy is astonished, impressions form him, he learns in play, he is surprised by seriousness. What is excellent is seldom found, more rarely esteemed. It is the height that stimulates us, not the steps; we gladly walk in the plain with our eyes on the peak. Only a part of art can be taught, the artist needs it complete. Whoever half-knows art is always in error and talks a lot; whoever possesses it fully likes only to act and talks rarely or at most late. The former have no secrets and no strength, their teaching is tasty like bread that has been baked, and is satiating for *one* day; but flour cannot be sown, and seed-corn should not be ground. Words are good, but they are not what is best. The best is not made clear through words. The spirit in which we act is the highest. Action is only understood and reproduced by the spirit. Nobody knows what he is doing when he acts rightly; but we are always conscious of what is wrong. He who only works with signs is a pedant, a hypocrite or a bungler. There are many of them, and they feel good when they are together. Their chatter holds back the pupil, and their persistent mediocrity brings alarm to those who are outstanding. The teaching of the genuine artist opens up meaning; for where words fail, action speaks. The genuine pupil learns how to unravel what is unknown from what is familiar, and approaches close to the master.'

'Enough!' the Abbé cried, 'the rest in due course. Now take a look at those cases.'

Wilhelm went over and read the inscriptions on the scrolls. He was surprised to find Lothario's, Jarno's and his own 'years of apprenticeship' set up there, among many others whose names were unknown to him.

'May I hope to be able to cast an eye upon the scrolls?'

'Nothing in this room is now under lock and key as far as you are concerned.'

'May I ask a question?'

'Without any hesitation! And you can expect a decisive answer if it concerns a matter which is, and should be, close to your heart.'

'Very well then! You strange, wise men whose glance penetrates into so many secrets, can you tell me whether Felix really is my son?'

'Blessings upon you for this question!' the Abbé cried, clapping his hands for joy: 'Felix is your son. By that most holy element that lies concealed among us, I swear to you, Felix is your son! And in her attitudes his late mother was not unworthy of you. Receive the dear child from our hands, turn round, and dare to be happy!'

Wilhelm heard a voice behind him, turned round and saw a child's face peeping roguishly through the curtains at the entrance; it was Felix. The boy at once hid himself playfully, on being seen. 'Come along out!' the Abbé cried. He came running, his father rushed forward towards him, took him in his arms and pressed him to his heart. 'Yes, I can feel it,' he exclaimed, 'you are mine! For what heavenly gift do I have to thank my friends! Where have you come from, my child, just at this moment?'

'Don't ask,' said the Abbé. 'May you be blessed, young man! Your years of apprenticeship are over; nature has absolved you.'

BOOK EIGHT

Chapter One

Felix had leapt into the garden, Wilhelm followed him with delight, a lovely morning revealed every object with fresh charm, and Wilhelm enjoyed the most serene of moments. The free, magnificent world around them was new to Felix, and his father was not much more familiar with the objects about which the little boy inquired repeatedly and without tiring. In the end they attached themselves to the gardener who had to recite the names and uses of a good many plants; Wilhelm was seeing nature by means of a new organ, and the curiosity and inquisitiveness of the child made him feel for the first time how little interest he had taken in things outside himself, with how little he was familiar and how little knowledge he had. It was only on this day, the most agreeable day in his life, that his own personal development seemed to be starting; he felt the need to instruct himself, just at the time when he was required to teach.

Jarno and the Abbé had disappeared; they came again in the evening and brought a stranger with them. Wilhelm went towards him with surprise, he did not trust his eyes, it was Werner who likewise hesitated before recognizing him. Both embraced each other most affectionately, and both could not conceal that they found each other changed. Werner maintained that his friend had become taller, stronger, straighter, more developed in his nature and pleasanter in his manner.—'I miss something of his old frankness,' he added.—'It will reveal itself again as soon as we have recovered from our first surprise,' Wilhelm said.

There was much to prevent Werner making an equally favourable impression on Wilhelm. The good man seemed to have regressed rather than progressed. He was much thinner than in the old days, his pointed face seemed to be more delicate and his nose to be longer, his forehead and the crown of his head were bald, his voice was clear, vehement and loud, while his hollow chest, drooping shoulders and colourless cheeks left no doubt that here was a thoroughgoing hypochondriac.

Wilhelm was modest enough to express himself in very moderate terms about this great change, whereas the other man gave full rein to his friendly joy. 'Truly,' he exclaimed, 'if you have used your time badly and, as I suspect, won nothing, you have none the less become a personality, one who can and must make his fortune; don't loiter about and squander this opportunity again! With your appearance you should be able to acquire for yourself a rich and beautiful heiress.'—'You are certainly true to your character,' Wilhelm rejoined with a smile. 'You have scarcely found your old friend again after a long time, when you already see him as a commodity, as an object for your speculation out of which some profit can be made.'

Jarno and the Abbé did not seem at all surprised at this scene of recognition and let the two friends go on at length about past and present events. Werner walked round his friend, turned him this way and that, almost making him feel embarassed. 'No, no,' he exclaimed, 'nothing like this has happened to me before, and yet I know very well that I am not deceiving myself. Your eyes have become deeper, your brow broader, your nose more refined and your mouth kinder. Just look at the way he stands! How everything fits and harmonizes! And how laziness thrives! As for myself, on the other hand, poor devil that I am'— he looked at himself in the mirror,—'if I hadn't made a great deal of money in all this time, there would be nothing to me at all.'

Werner had not received Wilhelm's last letter; their business was the strange business-house in conjunction with which Lothario intended to buy the property. It was this business that brought Werner here; he had not expected to encounter Wilhelm on his way. The lawyer came, the papers were produced, and Werner found the proposals fair. 'If you mean well with this young man, as it seems you do,' he said, 'see to it that our share is not diminished; it is up to my friend to decide whether to accept the property and apply a part of his wealth to it.' Jarno and the Abbé gave assurance that this reminder was not necessary. The matter had hardly been settled in general terms when Werner expressed a desire for a game of L'hombre; he was in fact in the habit of doing so, and could not get through an evening without gaming.

When the two friends were on their own after dinner, they questioned each other in a very lively manner about all the things they wanted to share with one another. Wilhelm spoke warmly of his position and of the good fortune of his reception among such excellent people. On the other hand Werner shook his head and said, 'It's true, you shouldn't believe anything except what you see with your own eyes! More than one obliging friend has asserted to me that you were living with a dissolute young nobleman, supplying him with actresses, helping him to get through his money, and that it was your fault that he was on bad terms with all his relations.'—'It would annoy me on my own account and also on behalf of these good people that we are so misunderstood,' Wilhelm rejoined, 'if my theatre career had not made me reconciled to every sort of malicious gossip. How should people judge our actions which are only known to them in an isolated and fragmentary manner and of which they only see a minimal part, because good and bad deeds take place on the quiet and all that sees the light of day is an indifferent manifestation. After all, actors and actresses are set upon raised boards, lights are lit on all sides of them, the whole work is finished in a few hours, but rarely does anyone actually know what he's to make of it.'

Then followed questions about the family, about boyhood friends and the home town. Werner recounted in great haste all the changes that had taken place and spoke about what was still in existence and still going on. 'The women at home are cheerful and happy,' he said, 'there's never any shortage of money. They spend half their lives dressing up and the other half showing themselves off when they are dressed up. They are as thrifty as is reasonable. My children promise to become clever boys. In my mind's eye I can already see them sitting and writing, and reckoning, running, negotiating and dealing; each one is to be provided as soon as possible with a trade of his own, and as far as our belongings are concerned, you will really enjoy contemplating these. When we have settled things about the estates, you must immediately come home with me, for it really does look as if you could intervene in human undertakings with some sense. Your new friends are to be commended for having put you on to the right track. I am a silly devil and am just beginning to notice how fond I am of you, as I can't take my eyes off you because you look so fine and well. For that really is a different figure from the portrait that you once sent to your sister and which caused a great squabble at home. Mother and daughter found the young gentleman most charming, with open neck, chest half-exposed, a big ruff and hair hanging down over it, a round hat, a little short waistcoat and loosely hanging long trousers, whereas I maintained that the costume was only a hair's breadth away from a clown's. But now you look like a human being, all you need is the plait that I should be glad if you would tie your hair into, otherwise some time on your travels you will be taken for a Jew and asked for customs dues and safe-conduct.'

Meanwhile Felix had come into the room and when no attention was paid to him he had lain down on the settee and gone to sleep. 'Who's that little creature?' asked Werner. At that moment Wilhelm did not have the courage to tell the truth nor the inclination to recount a still somewhat equivocal story to a man who by nature was anything but credulous.

The whole company now went on to the estate in order to inspect it and finalize the negotiations. Wilhelm did not allow Felix to leave his side and for the boy's sake took really lively pleasure in the anticipated ownership of the property. The child's craving for the cherries and berries that were about to ripen reminded him of his own childhood and of a father's multifarious duties to prepare, obtain and retain the pleasures of life for his family. With what interest he looked at the tree-plantations and the buildings! How keenly he gave thought to restoring what had been neglected and renewing what had decayed! He no longer looked at the world as does a bird of passage, he no longer considered a building to be a summer-house that has been quickly put together and which dries out before it is left again. Everything that he was thinking of investing was to increase for the boy's sake, and everything that he set up was to last for several generations. In this sense his years of apprenticeship were over, and with the feeling of paternity he had also acquired all the virtues of a citizen. He sensed this, and his joy was incomparable. 'Oh, how unnecessarily strict morality is,' he exclaimed, 'since nature in her charming way moulds us into everything that we ought to be. Oh, how strange are the requirements of civic society which in the first place confuses and misleads us and then demands more of us than nature herself! Alas, for any kind of education which destroys the most effective means of true development and directs us to the goal instead of bringing us happiness upon the way!'

Although he had already seen much in the course of his life, none the less human nature seemed to have become clear to him for the first time in his observations of the child. The theatre, like the world, had only appeared to him as a quantity of scattered dice, each one of which signifies sometimes more, sometimes less, and which certainly amount to a sum when they are added up. Here in the child a single cube lay before him, on whose many sides the value and the worthlessness of human nature had been so clearly engraved.

The child's desire to perceive more clearly grew every day. Once he had learnt that things have names, he wanted now to hear the name of everything; he indeed believed that his father must know everything, often pestered him with questions and gave him cause to inquire about objects to which he had formerly paid little attention. What is more, the innate drive to find out about the origin and end of things showed itself in the boy at an early stage. When he asked where the wind came from and where the flame went to, his father for the first time became really aware of his own limitations; he wanted to learn how far man might venture with his thoughts and what he might hope to account for to himself and to others. The child's strong feelings when he saw wrong being done to any living creature pleased the father greatly, as the indication of a noble spirit. The child violently hit the kitchen-maid who had been cutting up some pigeons. It is true, this pleasing conception was soon destroyed again when he found the boy killing frogs without mercy and pulling butterflies to pieces. This trait reminded him of so many people who appear to be most upright when their emotions are not involved and they are observing the actions of others.

The pleasant feeling that the boy was having such an agreeable and real influence on his existence was disturbed for a short while when Wilhelm noticed that really the boy was educating him more than he the boy. He did not find fault with the child at all, he did not lead him in a way that he did not take of his own accord, and even the bad habits which Aurelia had combatted all reasserted themselves, it seemed, after the death of this friend. The boy still never closed doors after himself, nor would he finish up what was on his plate, and he was never more content than when people condoned his taking food directly from the dish, or the way he could leave a full glass and drink out of the bottle. He was also very charming when he sat down in a corner with a book and very seriously said: 'I must study this learnèd stuff!', although he was still far from being able or willing to distinguish the letters of the alphabet.

When Wilhelm considered how little he had done for the child up to now and how little he was capable of doing, a disquiet arose in him which was in a position to outweigh his whole happiness. 'For are we men born so selfish,' he said to himself, 'that we can't possibly take on the care of anyone apart from ourselves? Am I not just on the same track with the boy as I was with Mignon? I drew the dear child to myself, her presence was agreeable to me, and yet I have neglected her most cruelly. What have I done about her educational development, which she longed for so much? Nothing! I left her to her own devices and to all the chance impressions to which she could be exposed in rough society; and then, has your heart ever bid you do the slightest thing for this boy who so attracted your attention before he could be so precious to you? It is no longer the time for me to be wasting my own years and the years of others; I must pull myself together and consider what I have to do for myself and the dear creatures to whom I am so closely bound by nature and inclination.'

Actually this monologue was only a preface to admitting to himself that he had already thought, made provision, sought and chosen; he could no longer hesitate to acknowledge it to himself. After frequently and vainly repeated grief at the loss of Mariane he felt only too clearly that he must look for a mother for the boy and that he would not find one more assuredly than in Theresa. He knew this excellent lady very well. Such a wife and helper seemed to be the only one to whom he and his dependants could be entrusted. Her noble-minded attraction to Lothario aroused no misgivings in him. They had been separated for ever by a strange fate, Theresa considered herself free and had spoken of marriage with indifference, it is true, but as of something that was taken for granted.

After thinking it over for a long time, he resolved to tell her all that he knew about himself. She should get to know him as he knew her, and he now began to think carefully about his own story; it seemed to him so empty of incident, and on the whole it appeared as if any confession would be of so little advantage to him that more than once he was on the point of giving up his intention. Finally he determined to ask Jarno for the scroll of his years of apprenticeship from the tower; the latter said: 'It is just the right time,' and Wilhelm received it.

It is a horrible feeling when a person with lofty aspirations consciously arrives at that point where he is to be given enlightenment about himself. All transitions are crises, and is not a crisis an illness? How reluctantly do we step before the mirror after an illness! We are aware of feeling better, but we see only the effect of the previous malady. In the meantime Wilhelm was sufficiently prepared, his position had already been revealed to him in lively terms, his friends had not exactly been sparing of him, and even if he did unroll the parchment with a certain haste, he none the less became more and more composed the further he read. He found the detailed story of his life depicted in large, sharp outlines; neither isolated events nor limited feelings confused his vision; general observations of a loving nature gave him pointers without putting him to shame, and for the first time he saw his own picture outside himself, admittedly not as in a mirror, a second self, but as in a portrait, another self: we do not admit to all the traits, it is true, but we are pleased that a thoughtful mind and a great talent should have wished to portray us in this way, that a picture of what we were still remains and that it can last longer than we ourselves.

Now Wilhelm busied himself, since this manuscript was bringing back all past circumstances to his memory, with drawing up the story of his life for Theresa, and he almost felt ashamed that he had nothing that could indicate purposeful activity which he might set up against her great virtues. Detailed though he was in his written account, he expressed himself briefly in the letter which he wrote to her; he asked her for her friendship and love, if this should be possible; he offered her his hand and begged her for a quick decision.

After some inward conflict as to whether he should first discuss this important matter with his friends, with Jarno and the Abbé, he decided to keep silent. He had made up his mind too firmly and the matter was too important to him, for him to have wished to submit it to the judgment even of the most sensible and excellent man; indeed, he even took the precaution of presenting his letter himself for the next post. Perhaps the thought that he had been observed, in fact directed, in so many circumstances of his life in which he had believed that he had been acting freely and in privacy, as seemed evident from the scroll, had given him a kind of unpleasant feeling, and now he wanted to address himself completely honestly, at least to Theresa's heart, and therefore he felt no misgivings at eluding his watchmen and overseers in this important point at least.

Chapter Two

The letter had only just been despatched when Lothario returned. Everybody was pleased that the important business that had been negotiated was now completed, and Wilhelm was waiting impatiently to find out how so many threads were in part to be newly tied and in part to be unravelled, and how his own situation was now to be determined with a view to the future. Lothario greeted them all most cordially; he was fully recovered and in cheerful mood, he had the appearance of a man who knows what he has to do and for whom there is no obstacle.

Wilhelm was unable to return the warmth of Lothario's greeting. He felt compelled to say to himself: 'This is the friend, the beloved and the fiancé of Theresa, and it is into his shoes that I am thinking of stepping. How can I ever obliterate or banish such an impression?'—If the letter had not already gone, he would perhaps not have dared to send it. Fortunately the initiative had already been taken, possibly Theresa had already made up her mind, and only distance still concealed a happy outcome with its veil. There would have to be a decision soon about gains and losses. He tried to calm himself down by means of all these considerations, but the beating of his heart was almost feverish. He could only devote a small amount of attention to the important business upon which to a certain extent the fate of his whole resources depended. Oh, how insignificant everything that surrounds us and belongs to us seems to be, from our point of view in moments of passion.

Fortunately for Wilhelm Lothario dealt with the business transaction in a generous spirit, and Werner acted promptly. With his emphatic acquisitiveness the latter was very pleased at the fine property which was to become his, or rather his friend's. Lothario for his part seemed to be thinking on quite different lines. 'I can't take as much pleasure about a piece of property as in its legality.'

'Well, good heavens!' cried Werner, 'isn't this property of ours legitimate enough?'

'Not altogether!' Lothario replied.

'Don't we provide our hard cash for it?'

'Agreed!' said Lothario; 'what is more, what I have in mind you will perhaps consider to be an empty scruple. No ownership strikes me as quite legitimate and tidy except when it gives its due portion to the state.'

'What?' said Werner, 'so you would really prefer it if our freely purchased estates were to be taxable?'

'Yes,' Lothario rejoined, 'to a certain extent; for it is solely through this equality with all other possessions that security of land-ownership arises. What fundamental reason can the peasant-farmer find nowadays, when so many concepts are in the balance, for regarding the nobleman's conditions of property owning as less justified than his own? Just this, that the nobleman is not encumbered with tax whereas this does bear down upon the farmer?'

'But what is the interest on our capital going to look like?' Werner answered.

'It wouldn't be any the worse,' Lothario said, 'if the state were to remit the hocus-pocus of feudal tenure in exchange for a small regular tax-payment and to allow us to deal with our estates as we liked, so that we were not compelled to keep our property together in big masses, and that we could divide it more equally among our children, in order that they could all be provided with vigorous and free activity, instead of having to bequeath to them only the limited and limiting privileges, and in order to enjoy these we always have to call up the spirits of our ancestors. How much happier men and women would be, if they could look around freely and choose now a worthy girl, now an excellent youth, without ulterior motives. The state would have more, perhaps better citizens and not be so often at a loss for heads and hands.'

'I can assure you,' said Werner, 'that I have never thought of the state in my life; I've only paid my taxes, tariffs and customs dues because it happened to be customary.'

'Well now,' said Lothario, 'I still hope to make a good patriot out of you; for just as he alone is a good father who serves his children first at table, so he alone is a good citizen who before any other expenditure puts on one side what he has to pay as his due to the state.'

Their particular business was not held up by general observations such as these, but on the contrary speeded up. When they had made quite a little progress with it, Lothario said to Wilhelm: 'I must now send you to a place where you are more needed than here: my sister entreats you to come to her as soon as possible; poor Mignon seems to be wasting away, and it is thought that your presence could perhaps still put a stop to the malady. Further, my sister has sent this letter on to me, and from this you will see how important it is for her.' Lothario handed a note to him. Wilhelm who had already felt very embarrassed while he was listening, at once recognized these rough pencillings as the Countess' handwriting, and did not know how to answer.

'Take Felix with you,' said Lothario, 'so that the children can keep each other company. You will have to set off early in the morning; my sister's coach, in which my people have come here, is still with us, I will give you horses for half the journey, then you can take the post-chaise. Let me wish you a cordial good-bye, and do convey many greetings on my behalf. In doing so, tell my sister that I shall see her again soon, and that she is in any case to get ready for some visitors. The friend of our great-uncle, Marchese Cipriani, is on the way here; he had hoped to meet the old man while he was still alive, and they were going to entertain each other with memories of earlier times and to enjoy together their common love of art. The Marchese was much younger than my uncle and owed him the major part of his educational development; we must do all we can in some measure to fill the gap which he will find, and we shall be able to do that best by means of a fairly large party of people.'

After this Lothario went to his room with the Abbé, Jarno having ridden away earlier; Wilhelm hurried to his room, he had nobody in whom he could confide, nobody through whose help he could have averted a step which he feared so much. The little servant came and requested him to pack, as they wanted to have the luggage arranged in the coach that night, in order to set off at the break of day. Wilhelm did not know what he should do; finally he exclaimed: 'I only want to see to it that I get out of this house; on the journey I must think what is to be done, and I can if need be stay on at the halfway point, send a messenger back, write what I don't trust myself to say, and then things can proceed as they please.' In spite of this resolve he spent a sleepless night; it was only a glance at Felix who was resting so peacefully that gave him some cheer. 'Oh!' he cried out, 'who knows what further trials await me, who knows how much past failings still torment me, and how often I am to be disappointed in plans for the future which are good and sensible! But preserve for me this treasure which I now possess, you Fate that either can or cannot be moved! If it were possible that this best part of me were to be destroyed before myself, that this heart could be torn from my heart, then good-bye to intelligence and reason, good-bye to all caring and provision, good-bye to you, instinct of conservation! Let everything be lost that distinguishes us from animals! And if it is not permissible to terminate voluntarily our sad days, may early madness put an end to conscious awareness before death, which destroys consciousness for ever, brings about the long night!'

He clasped the boy in his arms, kissed him, pressed him against himself and covered him with ample tears. The child awoke; his bright eye and friendly glance moved the father most strongly. 'What sort of a scene awaits me,' he exclaimed, 'if I am to introduce you to the beautiful unhappy Countess, if she presses you to her heart which your father has hurt so deeply! Must I not fear that she will push you away with a cry as soon as the contact with you renews her real or imagined pain?'

The coachman did not leave him time to think further or to make choices, he urged him before daybreak into the coach; then Wilhelm wrapped up Felix well, the morning was cold but clear, and for the first time in his life the child saw the sun rise. His surprise at the first fiery glimpse and at the growing strength of the light, his joy and his strange comments brought pleasure to the father and allowed him a glance into the mind of the boy before whom the sun was rising and hovering as if over a pure quiet lake.

In a small town the coachman changed horses and went back. Wilhelm at once took a room and now asked himself whether he should stay or go on. In this indecisiveness he ventured to look again at the note which up to now he had not ventured to read a second time; it contained the following words: 'Do send me your young friend soon! If anything, Mignon has taken a turn for the worse these last two days. Sad though the occasion is, I hope all the same to enjoy getting to know him.'

At first glance Wilhelm had not noticed the last phrase. He was startled by it and at once made up his mind that he did not wish to go. 'What?' he cried out, 'Lothario, who knows about the relationship, has not revealed to her who I am? She is not awaiting with composure an acquaintance whom she would prefer not to see again, she is expecting a stranger, and I step in! I can see her step back with a shudder, I can see her blush! No, I can't possibly go on to face this scene.' At that moment the horses were led out and put into harness; Wilhelm was determined to unpack and to stay there. He was in a great turmoil. When he saw a maid coming up the stairs to tell him that everything was ready, he quickly searched in his mind for a reason that should compel him to stay, and his eyes rested casually on the note which he was holding in his hand. 'For heaven's sake!' he cried out, 'what is that? It isn't the handwriting of the the Countess, but of the Amazon!'

The maid came in, asked him to come down and led Felix away with her. 'It is possible?' he exclaimed, 'is it true? What am I to do? To stay and wait and clear things up? Or to make haste? To make haste and rush into some involvement? You are on the way to her and can hesitate? You are to see her this evening and you want to shut yourself up in prison of your own free will? It is her handwriting, yes, it is! This handwriting is calling you, her coach is harnessed to lead you to her, and now the puzzle is solved: Lothario has two sisters. He knows of my connection with the one; how much I owe to the other is unknown to him. She also does not know that the wounded vagabond who owes her, if not his life, then his health has been received in her brother's house with such unmerited kindness.'

Felix who was rocking to and fro in the coach down below called: 'Father come! Do come! Look at the lovely clouds, the lovely colours!'—'Yes, I'm coming,' Wilhelm cried as he leaped down the stairs, 'and all the aspects of the sky which you still admire so much, dear child, are nothing in comparison with the sight which I am expecting.'

Sitting in the coach he now recalled all the circumstances to his mind. 'So this Natalie is Theresa's friend too! What a discovery, what hope and what prospects! How strange that the anxiety about hearing anything about the one sister could completely conceal from me the existence of the other!' With what happiness he looked at his Felix; he hoped for the boy as well as for himself the friendliest of receptions.

Evening approached, the sun had set, the road was not the best, the postilion was driving slowly, Felix had gone to sleep, and new worries and misgivings were arising in our friend's heart. 'What delusions and what notions are overcoming you!' he said to himself, 'an uncertain similarity in the handwriting all at once makes you sure and gives you the opportunity of imagining the strangest fairy-tale.' He took out the note again, and in the waning daylight he again believed he could recognize the Countess' handwriting; his eyes would not find in the detail what his heart had said to him all at once in general terms.—'So these horses are taking me to a dreadful scene! Who knows if in a few hours they will not again be in the process of transporting me back? And if I were only going to meet her alone! But perhaps her husband is present, and perhaps the Baroness! How changed I shall find her! Shall I be able to stand and face her?'

Only a faint hope that he might be going towards his Amazon could occasionally penetrate the dark imaginings. Night had fallen, the coach rattled into a courtyard and came to a halt; a servant with a flambeau stepped forward from a magnificent portal and came down the broad steps to the coach. 'You have been expected a long time,' he said, as he opened up the carriage-door. After he had got out Wilhelm took the sleeping Felix in his arms, and the first servant called to another one, who was standing with a light in the doorway: 'Take the gentleman straight to the Baroness.'

Quick as lightning there flashed through Wilhelm's mind: 'What good luck! Whether by intention or chance, the Baroness is here! I am to see her first! Presumably the Countess is already asleep! You kind spirits, help me so that the moment of greatest embarrassment may pass by in a tolerable manner!'

He entered the house and found himself in the most solemn, and, as he felt, the holiest place which he had ever visited. A dazzling lantern that was hanging down lit up a broad gently rising staircase which confronted him and divided into two sections on turning up above. Marble statues and busts stood on pedestals and were ranged in niches; some seemed familiar to him. Youthful impressions do not disappear, even in their smallest parts. He recognized a Muse that had belonged to his grandfather, not from its form and its value, it is true, but from an arm that had been restored and the newly added pieces of the dress. It was as if he were in a fairy-tale. The child's weight became heavy for him; he hesitated on the steps and kneeled down as if he wished to hold him more comfortably. Actually, however, he needed a moment to recover. He could scarcely get up again. The servant who was lighting the way for him wanted to relieve him of the child, but he could not be parted from him. Then he entered the ante-room, and he was even more surprised to see the familiar picture of the sick prince on the wall. He scarcely had time to cast a glance at it, and the servant directed him through a number of rooms into a private room. There behind a lampshade that was concealing her a woman was sitting and reading. 'Oh, if only it were she!' he said to himself at that decisive moment. He put down the child who seemed to awaken, and he thought of approaching the lady, but the child collapsed overcome with sleep; the woman stood up and advanced towards him. It was the Amazon! He could not contain himself, he fell upon his knees and exclaimed: 'It is she!' He took hold of her hand and kissed it with infinite delight. The child lay on the carpet between the two of them and slept gently.

Felix was put on to the settee, Natalie sat down close to him, and she asked Wilhelm to sit on the seat which was nearby. She offered him some refreshments which he refused, as he was only concerned to assure himself that it was she and to see exactly and to recognize again for certain her features that were obscured by the lampshade. She told him about Mignon's illness in general, that the child was gradually being consumed by some deep emotions, that with her great sensitiveness, which she hid, she often suffered severely and dangerously from convulsions of her poor heart, that this first organ of life often suddenly stood still in the case of unexpected emotions and that no trace of the wholesome movement of life could be felt in the good child's bosom. Once this terrifying convulsion had passed, nature's power again expressed itself in violent pulsings and this time terrified the child through excess, just as previously she had suffered through deficiency.

Wilhelm recalled a comparable scene of convulsions, and Natalie referred to the doctor who would discuss the matter further with him and explain in more detail why the child's friend and benefactor had been summoned at this time. 'You will find one unexpected change in her,' Natalie continued; 'she now wears women's clothes, for which she had formerly such a dislike.'

'How did you manage that?' Wilhelm asked.

'If it was something desirable, we owe it only to chance. Listen to what happened. You perhaps know that I always have a number of young girls around me whose minds I wish to direct towards what is good and right as they grow up beside me. They hear nothing from my lips except what I myself consider to be true, but I cannot and will not prevent them also from hearing from others error or prejudice such as is current in the world. If they ask me about this, I attempt as best I can to link the strange and unseemly ideas in some way to an idea that is right, in order to make them if not useful, at least harmless. For some time already my girls had heard from the farmers' children quite a lot about angels, Santa Claus and Christmas; they were said to appear at certain times, giving presents to good children and punishing naughty ones. The girls suspected that these must be people in disguise, and I then confirmed them in this, and without becoming much involved in interpretations I determined at the first opportunity to present them with a play on these lines. It happened that the birthday of twin sisters who had always been very well behaved was approaching; I promised that this time an angel would bring them the little presents which they had well deserved. They looked forward to the angel's appearance with great excitement. I had picked out Mignon for this part, and on the day in question she was appropriately dressed in a long, light, white gown. She even had a golden sash about her breast and a diadem of gold in her hair. At first I wanted to omit the wings, but the women who were dressing her up insisted on a pair of great golden pinions on which they could demonstrate their arts. So the strange figure stepped into the midst of the girls, a lily in one hand and a little basket in the other, and took me by surprise as well. "Here comes the angel," I said. The children all stepped back; finally they cried out: "It is Mignon!" and yet did not venture to come closer to the amazing tableau.

'"Here are your gifts," she said and handed over the little basket. The others collected around her, looked at her, touched her and questioned her.

'"Are you an angel?" one child asked.

'"I wish I were," Mignon replied.

'"Why are you carrying a lily?"

'"Were my heart as pure and open, then I would be happy."

'"How about the wings? Let's have a look!"

'And so she answered each innocent, simple question in a significant manner. When the curiosity of the little group had been satisfied and the first impression of her appearance had begun to wear off, there was the wish that she should have the costume taken off. She resisted this, took her zither, sat down on the high writing-desk and with astonishing charm sang a song.

> So, let me stay as I appear
> And let me keep this white dress on.
> I hasten to depart from here,
> And from your world I'll soon have gone.
>
> And when I'm there I'll rest a space
> And watch new vistas open wide;
> And then discard the husk of grace,
> Put sash and wings and wreath aside.
>
> For beings in their heavenly shape
> Are unaware of male or female,
> They have no need of cloak or drape,
> Expressing radiance without fail.
>
> My life was free from toil and care,
> And yet I felt deep grief and pain;
> I aged too soon in my despair;
> Make me for ever young again.

'I at once determined to let her keep the dress and to procure for her some more of the same kind,' Natalie continued, 'and it is these now that she is wearing too and in them, it seems to me, her personality takes on a quite different character.'

As it was already late, Natalie released the new arrival who left her not without anxiety. 'Is she married or not?' he thought to himself. He had feared that, whenever there was any movement, a door might open and the husband come in. The servant who conducted him to his room went away too quickly for Wilhelm to have had the courage to ask him about this relationship. Restlessness kept him awake for some time, and he occupied himself by comparing the picture of the Amazon with that of his new, present friend. They would not as yet completely converge; he had, as it were, created the former picture for himself, while the latter almost seemed to wish to remodel *him*.

Chapter Three

Next morning while everything was still calm and quiet he went to look around the house. The architectural style was the purest, most beautiful and most dignified that he had seen. 'After all,' he exclaimed, 'true art is like good company: it directs us in a very agreeable manner to recognize the standard according to which and by which our innermost being is shaped.' The impression which his grandfather's statues and busts made upon him was exceptionally agreeable. With yearning he hastened up to the picture of the sick prince, and he still found it attractive and moving. The servant opened several other rooms for him; he found a library, a natural history collection and a room with scientific exhibits. He felt so strange before all these objects. In the meantime Felix had woken up and had come hurrying after him; he was worried at the thought of how and when he would receive Theresa's letter; he was afraid of Mignon's expression and to some extent also of Natalie's. How different his present mood was from those moments when he had sealed up the letter to Theresa and was cheerfully dedicating himself completely to such a fine person.

Natalie had called him to breakfast. He entered a room where various neatly dressed girls, all apparently less than ten years old, were laying a table while an oldish person was bringing in various kinds of beverages.

Wilhelm looked attentively at a picture hanging above the settee; he felt obliged to take it to be Natalie's picture, unsatisfactory though this assumption was to him. Natalie came in, and the resemblance seemed to disappear completely. He was comforted to notice that the figure in the picture had a cross of an order on her breast, and he saw an identical cross on Natalie's breast.

'I have been looking at this portrait,' he said to her, 'and I am surprised to see how a painter can at one and the same time be so truthful and so wrong. In general the picture is very much like you, and yet these are neither your features nor your character.'

'What is rather more surprising,' Natalie replied, 'is that there is so much similarity; for it isn't my picture at all; it is the portrait of an aunt who even in her later years had a resemblance with myself when I was still a child. It was painted when she was about my age, and at first glance everybody thinks that they are looking at me. You should have known this excellent person. I owe her a great deal. Very poor health, perhaps too much preoccupation with herself, and at the same time an ethical and religious timidity prevented her from being to the world what she could have become in other circumstances. She was a light that shone only for a few friends, and in particular for me.'

'Would it be possible,' Wilhelm rejoined, for he had thought for a moment, since so many types of circumstances now seemed to be coinciding for him all at once, 'would it be possible that that beautiful, wonderful soul whose quiet confessions have been passed on to me too might be your aunt?'

'You have read the manuscript?' asked Natalie.

'Yes,' Wilhelm replied, 'with the greatest interest and not without an effect upon my whole life. What stood out most for me from this piece of writing was, if I may say so, the purity of life, not only her own but also of all that surrounded her, the independence of her nature and the impossibility for her of absorbing anything into her being that was not in harmony with her noble-minded and loving disposition.'

'In this respect,' Natalie answered, 'you are fairer and, I dare indeed say, more just to this beautiful personality than a number of others to whom this manuscript has also been entrusted. Every cultivated person knows to what extent he has to combat a certain coarseness in himself and in others, how much his development costs him, and to what a great degree in certain circumstances he only thinks of himself and forgets what he owes to others. How often a good person reproaches himself for not having acted sufficiently sensitively; and yet, if a fine personality is cultivated, indeed, if you like, over-cultivated, in all too sensitive and all too conscientious manner, the world seems to have no toleration or indulgence for him. But people of this kind are to our outer selves what ideals are within, models not to be imitated but to be aspired to. There is laughter at the cleanliness of Dutch women, but would our friend Theresa be what she is, if a similar idea were not always in her mind with regard to her house-keeping?'

'So in Theresa's friend,' Wilhelm exclaimed, 'I therefore find before me that Natalie who meant so much to the affections of that excellent relative, that Natalie who from childhood onwards was so sympathetic, loving and helpful! Only from among such a family could such a personality arise! What a prospect opens before me now that I can all at once command a view over your forefathers and the whole circle to which you belong!'

'Yes, indeed!' Natalie added, 'in a certain sense you could not be better informed about us than by means of aunt's essay; admittedly her liking for me caused her to say a lot of good things about me as a child. When people talk about a child, they never talk about the present state, but are always expressing their hopes.'

Meanwhile Wilhelm had quickly calculated that now he also had information about Lothario's origins and early years; the beautiful Countess appeared before him as a child with her aunt's pearls round her neck; he too had been so close to these pearls when her delicate, loving lips had come close to his own; he endeavoured to banish these charming memories with other thoughts. In his mind he went through the acquaintances that that piece of writing had procured for him. 'So I am in the worthy Uncle's house then! It isn't a house, it's a temple, and you are the estimable princess, in fact the presiding genius in person; I shall remember for the rest of my life the impression I had yesterday evening when I came in and found the old works of art from my earliest childhood standing before me again. I recalled the pitying marble-statues in Mignon's song; but these images did not have to grieve about me, they were looking at me with great seriousness and could link the earliest time in my life with the present moment. This old family treasure of ours, the joy of life to my grandfather, I now find set up here among so many other meritorious works of art, and I, whom nature made the favourite of this good old man, unworthy as I am, oh God, in what connections and company do I find myself!'

The young girls had been gradually leaving the room to attend to their own little affairs. Wilhelm, who had remained alone with Natalie, had to explain his last words to her more clearly. The discovery that a considerable part of the works of art on display had belonged to his grandfather gave rise to a very cheerful, sociable atmosphere. Just as he had been introduced to the house through the manuscript, so he now also found himself among his inheritance, as it were. Now he wanted to see Mignon; Natalie asked him to be patient until the doctor, who had been summoned out into the neighbourhood, should come back. It can easily be imagined that this was the same, small, active man whom we already know and who is also mentioned in the 'Confessions of a Beautiful Soul.'

'As I am in the midst of that family circle,' Wilhelm continued, 'the Abbé mentioned in that piece of writing is presumably the same strange, inexplicable man whom I met again in your brother's house after the most extraordinary events? Perhaps you can give me some further information about him?'

Natalie replied: 'There is a great deal one could tell about him; what I am most familiar with is the influence which he has had on our education. He was convinced, at least for a time, that education must be associated only with inclination; what he now thinks I can't say. He maintained that as far as human beings were concerned, activity counted above all else, and that we can do nothing without having the predisposition to it, the instinct which drives us on. "It is recognized," he used to say, "that poets are born and not made, this is admitted in all the arts because it has to be, and because those activities of the human mind can apparently scarcely be imitated; but when we look at it closely, every capacity, including even the slightest, is innate, and there are no undetermined capacities. It is only our ambivalent and sporadic education that makes people uncertain; it arouses wishes instead of stimulating instincts, and instead of assisting real potentialities, it directs effort to objects which frequently are not in accord with the personality that is striving after them. A child and a young person who take the wrong turning on the path they have mapped out for themselves are more sympathetic to me than many people who make their way correctly, but on an alien path. If the former, either by themselves or with guidance, find the right path, that is, the one which is congenial to them by nature, they will never leave it, whereas the latter are every moment in danger of shaking off a strange yoke and giving themselves up to unqualified freedom."'

'It is strange,' said Wilhelm, 'that this remarkable man has also taken an interest in me and, if he has not led me, as it seems, has at least for a time strengthened me in my errors. To learn how he will in future take responsibility for making fun of me, as it were, in combination with several others, I shall presumably have to wait patiently.'

'I have no complaints about this whim, if that's what it is,' said Natalie, 'for certainly I have come off best in this respect amongst my brothers and sisters. I also don't see how my brother Lothario could have been educated better; only perhaps my good sister, the Countess, ought to have been treated differently, perhaps rather more seriousness and strength could have been added to her character. What is to happen to our brother Friedrich just doesn't bear thinking of; I fear that he will become the sacrificial victim of these pedagogic experiments.'

'You have another brother?' cried Wilhelm.

'Yes,' replied Natalie, 'and what is more, his is a very merry, frivolous temperament, and as he has not been prevented from travelling about in the world, I don't know what is to become of this easy-going and disorderly fellow. I haven't seen him for a long time. The one thing that comforts me is that the Abbé and my brother's Society in particular are informed at all times as to where he is and what he is doing.'

Wilhelm was about to probe Natalie's thoughts concerning

these paradoxes as well as to elicit information from her about the secret Society when the doctor came in and after preliminary greetings at once began to talk about Mignon's condition.

Natalie then took Felix by the hand and said that she would go with him to Mignon and prepare the child for her friend's appearance.

The doctor was now alone with Wilhelm and continued: 'I have strange things to tell you, which you are scarcely expecting. Natalie is leaving us on our own so that we can speak more freely of things which, although I have only been able to learn about them from her, none the less could not be discussed so freely in her presence. The strange temperament of the child whom we are now talking about consists almost entirely of a deep yearning; I might almost say, the longing to see her native country again and the longing for you, my friend, are the only earthly things about her; both stretch into infinity, both objects are unattainable to this unique disposition. Her home may be in the Milan area, and she was abducted from her parents at a very early age by a company of acrobats. It is not possible to find out anything more definite from her, partly because she was too young to be able to give precise information about the place and her name, but in particular because she has made a vow not to reveal any closer details about her home and her origins to a living soul.

For those very people who found her when she was lost and to whom she described her home so exactly, with such pressing requests, took her away with them all the more hastily, and in the inn at night, when they believed that the child was already asleep, they joked about the good catch they had made and asserted that she would not find the way back again. At that the poor creature was overcome by terrible despair in the course of which the Mother of God appeared to her and assured her that she would take care of her. She then swore to herself a sacred vow that she would trust nobody else in future, nor tell anyone her story and that she would live and die in the hope of divine intervention. Even what I am telling you now she did not confide to Natalie in so many words; our dear friend has pieced it together from separate statements, songs and child-like indiscretions which reveal precisely what they wish to conceal.'

Now Wilhelm was able to account for many a song and many a saying of this dear child. He asked his friend in the most pressing terms not to withhold from him anything that he knew about the strange songs and confessions of the unique creature.

'Oh!' said the Doctor, 'prepare yourself for an extraordinary confession, for a story in which you are much involved without your remembering it, a story which, as I fear, is a matter of life and death for this good soul.'

'Do tell me,' Wilhelm replied, 'I am extremely impatient.'

'Do you remember a secret, nocturnal woman visitor after the performance of *Hamlet*?' the Doctor said.

'Yes, I well remember the occasion!' Wilhelm exclaimed in some confusion, 'but I did not think that I should be reminded of it just now.'

'Do you know who she was?'

'No! You shock me! For heaven's sake, surely not Mignon? Who was it? Tell me!'

'I don't know myself.'

'Not Mignon then?'

'No, certainly not! But Mignon was on the point of going to you when with horror she was compelled to observe from a corner that a rival was forestalling her.'

'A rival!' Wilhelm cried out, 'tell me more! You are altogether bewildering me.'

'Be content that you can learn of these consequences from me so quickly,' the Doctor said. 'Natalie and myself, who after all are only able to be involved in a fairly remote way, were tormented long enough until we had as much insight as this into the confused condition of this dear creature whom we wanted to help. Frivolous chatter of Philine and the other girls, together with a certain little song, had aroused her attention and made attractive to her the thought of spending a night with her loved one, without her being able to envisage by this anything further than a trusting, happy repose. The affection for you, my friend, had already become lively and powerful in her good heart, and the dear child had already rested in your arms in face of many a paroxysm of suffering; now she desired this happiness in its completeness. Sometimes she resolved to ask for it in a friendly way, sometimes a secret terror would hold her back once more. Finally the cheerful evening party and the mood induced by the frequent partaking of wine gave her the courage to try the bold venture of slipping in with you that night. She had gone ahead so that she could hide herself in the unlocked room, only just as she had come up the stairs she heard a noise; she concealed herself and saw a female figure in white slip into your room. You yourself came soon afterwards, and she heard the big bolt being put on.

'Mignon suffered unbearable torment, all the vigorous emotions of passionate jealousy were combined with the unrecognized demands of an obscure desire and played havoc with her youthful temperament. Her heart, which up to that point had been beating animatedly with yearning and expectation, all at once began to falter and felt like a lead weight in her bosom, she couldn't get her breath, she didn't know how to protect herself. She heard the old man's harp, hurried up to him in the attic and spent the night at his feet amid terrible convulsions.'

The Doctor paused a moment, and as Wilhelm kept silent, he went on: 'Natalie has assured me that in her whole life nothing had terrified and affected her as much as the child's condition while giving this account; indeed our noble-minded friend reproached herself for having elicited these confessions with her questions and hints and for having recalled so cruelly the intense sufferings of the dear girl.

'"The good creature had scarcely got to this point in her narrative, or rather in her answers to my mounting questions," so Natalie told me, "when all at once she collapsed before me and with her hand on her bosom complained of the return of the pain of that terrible night. She writhed like a snake on the ground, and I had to summon up all my composure in order to think of and apply the remedies I knew for a mind and body in these circumstances."'

'You put me in a somewhat anxious frame of mind,' Wilhelm cried, 'since you make me so keenly aware of the repeated wrongs I have inflicted on the dear creature, just at the moment when I am due to see her again. If I am to see her, why do you deprive me of the confidence needed to approach her freely? And am I to confess to you that since she is feeling like this, I don't see what good my presence will do? If you are convinced as a doctor that this double craving has undermined her nature to such an extent that she is threatening to take her life, why should I renew her sufferings by my presence and perhaps hasten her end?'

'My friend,' replied the Doctor, 'where we can't help, we are obliged none the less to alleviate, and I can give impressive examples of the extent to which the presence of a loved object can deprive the imagination of its destructive force and convert desire into quiet contemplation. Everything in moderation! For in the same way presence can rekindle an expiring passion. See the dear child, behave in a friendly way, and let us await what comes of it.'

Natalie returned just then and asked Wilhelm to follow her to Mignon. 'She seems to be entirely happy with Felix and will give our friend a good reception, I hope.' Wilhelm followed not without some reluctance; he had been deeply moved by what he had heard and feared a passionate scene. When he went in, exactly the opposite occurred.

Mignon was sitting wearing a long white dress, her abundant brown hair partly in loose curls and partly tied up, and she had Felix on her lap and was pressing him to her heart; she looked just like a departed spirit, and the boy like life itself; it seemed as if heaven and earth were embracing. With a smile she stretched out her hand to Wilhelm and said: 'Thank you for bringing back the child to me; they had made off with him, God knows how, and I haven't been able to go on living since then. As long as my heart still has any needs on earth, he shall fill the gap.'

The calm with which Mignon had received her friend gave the group great satisfaction. The Doctor asked Wilhelm to see her frequently and requested that she should be kept on an even keel both in body and in mind. He himself departed, and promised to come again shortly.

Wilhelm could now observe Natalie in her own circle: nothing better could be desired than to live by her side. Her presence had the most felicitous influence on young girls and women of various ages, some of whom lived in her house while others from the neighbourhood came more or less to visit her.

'Am I right in thinking that the course of your life has always been very smooth?' Wilhelm once said to her, 'for the description which your aunt gives of you as a child still seems to fit, unless I am mistaken. One can feel that you have never been confused. You have never been compelled to take a step back.'

'I owe that to my uncle and the Abbé,' Natalie replied, 'who were so good at judging my peculiarities. From my childhood days I can scarcely remember having a more vivid impression than seeing what it was people needed everywhere and feeling an irresistible impulse to make good these needs. The child that had not yet learnt to walk, the old man no longer capable of standing on his feet, a wealthy family's longing for children, the inability of a poor family to maintain their own children, every quiet aspiration to a vocation, the impulse to develop a talent, the potentiality for a hundred necessary little talents—my eyes seemed destined by nature to discover these everywhere. I noticed things that nobody had drawn my attention to; but it also seemed as if I had only been born in order to see them. The attractions of inanimate nature, to which so many people are extremely responsive, had no effect on me, and the attractions of art had almost less; it was, and still is, my most pleasant experience to find in my mind some compensation, some means, some help as soon as any shortcoming or need in the world was revealed to me'.

'If I saw a poor man in rags, I thought of the superfluous clothes I had seen hanging in the wardrobes of members of my family; if I saw children who were pining away without being cared for or tended, I would remember this or that woman whom I had noticed to be bored in spite of riches and comfort; if I saw a lot of people confined in a narrow space, I thought that they should be given the use of the large rooms of many houses and palaces. This way of looking at things was quite natural for me, without the slightest reflection, so that I behaved as a child in the oddest way and embarrassed people with the strangest offerings. Another peculiarity was that it was only with difficulty and at a late stage that I came to see money as a means of satisfying needs; all my benefactions consisted of natural produce, and I know that I was laughed at often enough. Only the Abbé seemed to understand me, he met me half-way every time, it was he who taught me to know myself and to be acquainted with these wishes and inclinations, and told me how to fulfil them in an appropriate manner.'

'Then have you also accepted those strange men's principles in the education of your little company of women?' Wilhelm asked. 'Do you also allow each personality to develop as it pleases? Do you also let them arrive happily at their objective, or get unhappily lost on the wrong track?'

'No!' said Natalie, 'this way of dealing with people would be entirely against my convictions. Unless you help in the moment of need, it seems to me you never do help; unless you give counsel at the time it is needed, you never do provide counsel. It seems to me just as necessary to formulate certain laws which give life a certain stability and to impress them upon children. Yes, I would almost like to maintain that it is better to err according to rules than to err when we are driven this way and that by the caprice of our temperament, and as I see people, there always seems to be in their nature a gap which can only be filled by a distinctly formulated law.'

'So your way of behaving is therefore completely different from that observed by our friends?' said Wilhelm.

'Yes!' Natalie rejoined. 'However, this shows you the incredible tolerance of these men, the fact that they don't interfere at all with me either as I go on my way, precisely because it is my way, but co-operate in everything that I could wish for.'

We will postpone until another occasion a more detailed account of the way Natalie managed the children.

Mignon often wanted to be in the company of the others, and

they were all the happier to grant this to her as she seemed
to be getting used to Wilhelm again gradually, to be opening
her heart to him and altogether to be becoming more cheerful
and vivacious. When they went for walks she liked to take his
arm, as she easily became tired. 'Now,' she said, 'Mignon no
longer climbs and jumps, and yet she still feels a desire to walk
off over the mountain tops and to stride from one house to
another, and from one tree to the next. How enviable the birds
are, when they build their nests so neatly and cosily!'

It had now become the usual thing for Mignon to invite her
friend to the garden again and again. If he was busy or not to be
found, Felix had to take his place, and if the dear girl seemed on
some occasions to be quite remote from earthly life, at other times
she clung again firmly, so to speak, to father and son, and
appeared to fear separation from them more than anything else.

Natalie seemed thoughtful. 'We have been trying to encourage
the poor dear heart to unfold again through your presence;
whether we have done well in this, I don't know.' She was
silent and seemed to be expecting Wilhelm to say something. It
also occurred to him that in the present circumstances Mignon
would be most hurt at his association with Theresa; only in his
uncertainty he did not trust himself to say anything about this
plan; he did not conceive that Natalie was informed of it.

No more could he pursue the discussion with freedom of spirit
when noble-minded Natalie talked about her sister, praising her
good qualities and commiserating on her position. He was not a
little embarrassed when Natalie announced to him that he would
soon see the Countess here. 'Her husband now has nothing
in mind apart from replacing the late Count[1] in the community,
and supporting this great institution and building it up further
by means of insight and activity. He is coming to us with her
with a kind of leave-taking in view; afterwards he will visit
the various places where communities of the brethren have been
set up; it seems as if he is being treated according to his own
wishes; and I almost believe that he will venture on a voyage
to America with my poor sister, in order to be really like his
predecessor; and as he is already almost convinced that he is
nearly a saint, the wish to be finally distinguished as a martyr as
well may possibly hover before his soul on occasion.'

---

[1] Count von Zinzendorf, who died in 1760. (Tr.)

Chapter Four

Up to now they had talked about Miss Theresa and mentioned her in passing often enough, and almost every time Wilhelm was about to confess to his new friend that he had offered his heart and hand to that excellent lady. A certain feeling that he could not declare himself, held him back; he hesitated so long until in the end Natalie said to him, with that heavenly, modest and cheerful smile that people were accustomed to see on her countenance: 'So in the end I've got to break the silence after all and force myself into your confidence! Why, my friend, do you make a secret out of an affair which is so important to you and which concerns me so closely? You have offered your hand in marriage to my friend; I am not intervening in this matter without due cause, here is my authority! Here is the letter which she has written to you and which she sends to you through me.'

'A letter from Theresa!' he exclaimed.

'Yes, sir, and your fate is decided. You are happy. Let me congratulate you and my friend.'

Wilhelm fell silent and stared ahead. Natalie looked at him; she noticed that he turned pale. 'Your happiness is a powerful feeling,' she continued, 'it assumes the shape of terror and robs you of language. My interest is none the less cordial because it still allows me to express myself in words. I hope you will be grateful, for I may tell you that my influence on Theresa's decision was not slight; she asked my advice, and strangely enough you happened to be here, I could happily overcome the few doubts that my friend was still nurturing, and messengers went rapidly back and forth; here is her decision! Here is the development! And now you are to read all her letters, you are to cast a free, clear eye upon the beautiful heart of your fiancée.'

Wilhelm unfolded the letter which she had handed to him unsealed; it contained the friendly words:

'I am yours, as I am and as you know me. I call you mine, as you are and as I know you. Any changes in ourselves and in our relationship that are caused by the married state we shall be able to deal with by means of good sense, cheerfulness and goodwill. As we are brought together not by passion, but by inclination and trust, we are risking less than a thousand other couples. I am sure you will pardon me if at times I remember my old friend with cordial feeling; in return I am willing to press your son to my heart as a mother. If you wish to share my little house with me straightaway, you are lord and master, and in the meantime the purchase of the estate is being completed. I should be glad if no new arrangements were made there without my being consulted, in order to demonstrate at once that I deserve the confidence which you accord to me. Good-bye, dear, dear friend! Dear fiancé, dear husband! Theresa presses you to her breast in hope and in joy of life. My friend will tell you more, will tell you everything.'

Wilhelm, for whom this note had completely evoked his Theresa again, had also become his former self once more. While he had been reading it, rapid thoughts raced through his mind. He was horrified to discover in his heart vigorous traces of an affection for Natalie; he reproached himself, he declared any such thought to be nonsense, he imagined Theresa in her whole perfection, he read the letter again, he became cheerful, or rather he recovered to such an extent that he could appear to be cheerful. Natalie laid the correspondence before him, and we wish to select some passages from these letters.

After Theresa had described her fiancé in her own way, she went on:

'That is how I imagine the man to be who is now offering me his hand. How he thinks of himself, you will find out at some future time from the papers in which he describes himself to me quite openly; I am convinced that I shall be happy with him.'

'As far as social class is concerned, you know what my thoughts have always been on this subject. Some people feel the discrepancies of outer circumstances to a terrible degree and cannot overcome them. I don't wish to persuade anybody, just as I like to act according to my own convictions. I don't think of setting any example, though I do not act myself without example. I am afraid only of inner discrepancies, a container that is not appropriate for what it is intended to hold; a lot of show with little pleasure, riches with avarice, noble birth with coarseness, youth with pedantry, necessity with ceremony, these are the circumstances which could destroy me, though the world may hall-mark and esteem them as it will.'

'When I hope that we shall be well matched, I am basing my wish primarily on the fact that he is like you, dear Natalie, whom I esteem and respect so infinitely much. Yes, he has from you the spirit of noble seeking and aspiration for what is better, by means of which we bring forth the goodness that we believe we shall find. How often have I not blamed you privately because you treated this or that person differently than I would have done and because in a particular case you behaved differently, and yet the outcome usually showed that you were right. "If all we do is take people as they are," you would say, "we shall make them worse; if we treat them as if they were what they ought to be, we shall lead them to that place where they are to be led." I can neither see nor act like that, I know very well. Insight, order, propriety, these are my affair. I still need to remember what Jarno said: "Theresa trains her pupils, Natalie educates hers." Indeed, he went so far once as to deny me completely the three fine qualities of faith, love and hope. "Instead of faith she has insight," he said, "Instead of love tenacity, and instead of hope trust." I will also gladly admit to you that before I knew you I knew nothing in the world worthier than clarity and good sense; your presence alone has convinced, invigorated and overcome me, and I am happy to allow precedence to your beautiful, noble-minded soul. I look up to my friend too in the same spirit; his life-story is an eternal seeking without finding; but he is endowed not with empty seeking, but with a marvellous, confident searching, he thinks that others can give him what can only come from himself. And so, my love, my clarity of mind does me no harm on this occasion either; I know my husband to be better than he knows himself, and I respect him all the more for it. I can see him, but I cannot survey the whole of him, and all my insight is not adequate enough to let me surmise what he is capable of. Whenever I think of him, his picture is always mingled with yours, and I don't know how I can deserve to belong to two such people. But I wish to deserve it through doing my duty, and through fulfilling what can be expected and hoped of me.'

'You ask if I think of Lothario? Vividly, and daily. I cannot imagine for a moment that he might not be one of the company that surrounds me in my mind's eye. Oh, how sorry I am for the excellent man, who is related to me through a youthful error, that nature has wished him to be so close to you. Indeed, someone like yourself would be more deserving of him than myself. I would be able to, I would have to relinquish him to you. Let us be for him whatever is possible until he finds a wife who is worthy of him, and when this happens too, let us be together and stay together.'

'But what will our friends say now?' Natalie began.—

'Your brother knows nothing about it?'—'No, just as little as your people, this time the matter has only been discussed among us women. I don't know what fanciful notions Lydia has been putting into Theresa's head; she seems to mistrust the Abbé and Jarno. Lydia has induced in her at least some suspicions against certain secret associations and plans which I know about in a general way, but into which I have never thought of probing, and at this decisive step in her life she didn't wish anyone apart from myself to have any influence on her. She had already come to an agreement with my brother at an earlier stage that they would simply inform each other about their marriages and not seek each other's advice.'

Natalie now wrote a letter to her brother, she invited Wilhelm to add a few words, Theresa had asked her to do this. They were about to seal the letter when Jarno unexpectedly announced himself. He was received in the most friendly fashion, he too appeared to be very cheerful and jocular, and finally he could not refrain from saying: 'Actually I have come here to bring you some very strange, but pleasant news concerning our Theresa. You have criticized us more than once, beautiful Natalie, for concerning ourselves about so many things; but now you see how good it is to have spies everywhere. Make a guess, and let us see how acutely you discern now1!'

The complacency with which he spoke these words and the roguish mien with which he looked at Wilhelm and Natalie convinced them both that their secret was revealed. Natalie replied, smiling: 'We are cleverer than you think, we have already put down on paper the solution of the puzzle even before this was presented to us.'

With these words she handed to him the letter for Lothario, and was satisfied to confront in this way the little surprise and confusion that had been intended for them. Jarno took the letter in some surprise, just skimmed through it, was astonished, dropped it out of his hand and looked at them with wondering eyes and an expression of surprise, even of terror, which was not often to be seen on his features. He did not say a word.

Wilhelm and Natalie were not a little taken aback. Jarno paced up and down in the room. 'What am I to say?' he exclaimed, 'or shall I say it? It can't remain a secret, the confusion is unavoidable. So one secret in exchange for another, then! Surprise for surprise! Theresa is not her mother's daughter! The obstacle has been removed: I have come here to ask you to prepare the fine girl for a union with Lothario.'

Jarno saw the consternation of the two friends who cast their eyes down to the ground. 'This is one of those cases,' he said, 'which can be borne least well in company. What each one has to think about it, is best done in solitude; I at least request for myself an hour's leave.' He hurried into the garden, and Wilhelm followed him automatically, but at a distance.

After an hour had gone they came together again. Wilhelm began speaking, and said: 'At other times, when I lived without purpose and plan in an easy, indeed frivolous manner, friendship, love, affection and trust came to me with open arms, indeed they pressed upon me; now that it is a serious matter, fate seems to go another way with me. The decision to offer Theresa my hand is possibly the first one to come quite clearly from within myself. I thought out my plan, my intellect was completely in agreement with it, and all my hopes were fulfilled when the lovely girl consented. Now the strangest destiny knocks down my outstretched hand. Theresa stretches out her hand to me from afar, as if in a dream, I can't grasp it, and the beautiful image leaves me for ever. So good-bye, you fair image, and you images of most ample bliss that are gathered around!'

He paused for a moment, looking ahead, and Jarno was about to speak. 'Let me say something more,' Wilhelm interposed; 'for after all the die which is being cast is to settle my whole destiny. At this moment I am being helped by the impression which Lothario's presence made upon me when I first met him, an impression which has remained lasting for me. This man merits every kind of affection and friendship, and no friendship is conceivable which does not involve self-sacrifice. For his sake I found it easy to delude an unhappy girl, for his sake it is to be possible for me to renounce the most estimable fiancée. Go and tell him the strange story, and tell him what I am prepared to do.'

Jarno replied to this: 'In such cases, as I see it, everything falls into place so long as people don't hurry too much. Let us not take any step without Lothario's consent! I will go to him. Wait quietly for my return or for letters from him.'

He rode off and left the two friends behind in very great sadness. They had time to recapitulate this event in more than one way and to make their comments on it. Only now did it occur to them that they had accepted this strange explanation so directly from Jarno and had not inquired about the precise circumstances. In fact, Wilhelm was even willing to have some doubts; but their surprise, indeed their confusion, became most acute when on the next day a messenger from Theresa arrived, bringing the following peculiar letter to Natalie:

'Strange as it may seem, I must none the less straightaway send another letter after my previous one and implore you to send my fiancé to me in haste. He shall be my husband, whatever plans are being made to rob me of him. Give him the enclosed letter. Only not in the presence of any witness, whoever it may be.'

The letter to Wilhelm ran as follows: 'What will you think of your Theresa if all of a sudden she presses passionately for a union which seemed to have been initiated only by calmest reason? Don't let anything put you off setting out immediately you receive this letter! Come, my dear, dear friend who are now threefold beloved, since attempts are being made to deprive me of your possession or at least to make it difficult!'

'What's to be done?' Wilhelm cried, when he had read this letter.

'In no other case have my heart and my reason kept so silent as in this one,' Natalie added after some thought; 'I wouldn't know what to do, just as I don't know what to advise.'

'Could it be that Lothario himself knows nothing about it,' Wilhelm exclaimed vehemently, 'or if he does know about it, that together with ourselves he is the plaything of hidden plans? Did Jarno make up a fairy-tale on the spur of the moment after he had seen our letter? Would he have said something different to us, if we had not been so hasty? What can be intended? What sort of purposes can there be? What sort of a plan does Theresa mean? It's true, it cannot be denied, Lothario is surrounded by secret activities and connections, I have experienced myself that people are actively at work, that they concern themselves in a certain sense for the actions and destinies of a number of people and are in a position to direct them. I understand nothing of the ultimate objects of these secrets, but I can see only too clearly this latest intention to take Theresa from me. On the one hand these people depict for me Lothario's possible happiness, perhaps only for appearances' sake, on the other I see my beloved, my revered fiancée who summons me to her bosom. What shall I do? What shall I leave undone?'

'Just a little patience!' said Natalie, 'just a little time to think things over! In this strange connection I know only this much: that we should not be in too much of a hurry over something that is irredeemable. Persistence and sense will support us against a fairy-tale or a contrived plan; an explanation must come soon as to whether the business is true or whether it's an invention. If my brother really does hope to be united with Theresa, it would be cruel to deprive him for ever of a happiness at the moment when it appears before him in so propitious a manner. Let us just wait to see whether he knows something about it, whether he himself believes and hopes!'

Fortunately a letter from Lothario came to give support to these reasons for her advice: 'I am not sending Jarno back again,' he wrote: 'some lines in my handwriting will mean more to you than the most detailed account from any messenger. I am sure that Theresa is not her mother's daughter, and I cannot give up the hope of possessing her until she is convinced as well, and then decides with calm consideration between me and our friend. I beg you, don't let him go from your side! The happiness, the life of a brother depend upon this. I promise you, this uncertainty won't last long.'

'You see how things are,' she said to Wilhelm in a friendly manner; 'give me your word of honour that you won't leave the house!'

'I give you my word!' he exclaimed, offering her his hand; 'I will not leave this house against your wishes. I thank God and my guardian angel that I am being guided this time, and moreover by you.'

Natalie wrote to Theresa giving her a complete account and explained that she would not let their friend go from her; at the same time she enclosed Lothario's letter.

Theresa replied: 'I am not a little surprised that Lothario himself has been convinced; for he won't dissimulate to his sister to this extent. I am annoyed, very annoyed. It is better for me not to say anything further. It will be best for me to come to you as soon as I have made some arrangement about poor Lydia who is being treated very badly. I am afraid we have all been deceived, and are being deceived in such a way so that we shall never get things straight. If our friend saw things as I do, he would slip away from you after all and would fling himself upon the affections of his Theresa, whom nobody should then take away from him; but I am afraid that I am to lose him and not regain Lothario. Lydia is snatched from Lothario, while the latter is shown from afar the possibility of possessing me. I will not say anything further, the confusion will grow even greater. Time may tell whether in the meantime the noblest situation may be so distorted, undermined and thrown into confusion that even when everything becomes clear again, there is nothing further to be done. If my friend does not tear himself away, I shall come in a few days in order to look him up at your house and to hold him fast. You are surprised how this passion has taken hold of your Theresa. It is not a passion, it is a conviction that as Lothario could not become mine, this new friend will be the happiness of my life. Tell him this in the name of the little boy who sat with him underneath the oak-tree and was pleased to receive his sympathetic interest! Tell it to him in the name of Theresa who received his proposal with heartfelt openness! My first dream, of how I would live with Lothario, has withdrawn far from my mind; the dream of the way I have been thinking of living with my new friend is still fully before me. Am I thought so little of that people believe that it is an easy matter to exchange the former for the latter again on the spur of the moment?'

'I'm depending upon you,' Natalie said to Wilhelm as she gave him Theresa's letter. 'You won't take flight from me. Consider that you hold my life's happiness in your hand! My life is so closely bound and intertwined with my brother's life that he is unable to feel any sorrows that I don't feel and no joy that does not also make for my happiness. Yes, I can certainly say that through him alone have I felt that the heart can be moved and uplifted, and that there can be in the world happiness, love and a feeling that provides satisfaction beyond all need.'

She paused, Wilhelm took her hand and called out: 'Oh, do continue! It is the right time for true, mutual trust; we have never needed so much to know each other more closely.'

'Yes, my friend!' she said smiling, with her quiet, gentle, indescribable sublimity, 'it is perhaps not untimely for me to tell you that everything that is called and presented to us as love by so many books and by the world at large has always seemed to me to be only a fairy-tale.'

'Have you not been in love?' Wilhelm exclaimed.

'Never or always!' Natalie replied.

Chapter Five

During this conversation they had been walking up and down in the garden; Natalie had plucked various strangely shaped flowers which were completely unknown to Wilhelm and whose names he inquired about.

'I don't expect you can surmise whom I am picking this bunch of flowers for?', Natalie said. 'It is intended for my uncle, whom we are to pay a visit. The sun is shining now so brightly towards the Room of the Past, I must take you there this very moment, and I never go there without taking with me some of the flowers which my uncle particularly liked. He was a strange man and capable of the most peculiar impressions. He had a definite liking for certain plants and animals, for certain people and localities, indeed even for some kinds of stone, and it was a liking that could seldom be explained. "If I had not resisted my own inclinations from childhood onwards", he often used to say, "if I had not endeavoured to train my intellect along broad and general lines, I should have become the most limited and most unbearable person; for nothing is more unbearable than curtailed peculiarity in someone from whom a clear, appropriate form of activity can be demanded." And yet he had himself to confess that he would as it were be losing his life's spirit if he did not indulge himself from time to time and allow himself to enjoy spontaneously things that he could not always praise and excuse. "It isn't my fault," he said, "if I haven't been completely able to reconcile my impulses and my reason." On such occasions he used to tease me and to say: "Natalie can indeed be extolled as blessed, since her nature does not demand anything except what the world desires and needs."'

While these words were being spoken they had arrived again at the main building. She led him through a spacious corridor towards a door in front of which were two sphinxes of granite. The door itself was a little narrower at the top than lower down, in the Egyptian manner, and the bronze leaves of the double door prepared one for a serious, indeed an awe-inspiring sight. What a pleasant surprise it was therefore when this expectation was resolved into pure serenity on entering a room in which art and life removed every memory of death and the grave. Appropriately designed archways were let into the walls, and in them were sarcophagi of considerable size; in the pillars in between could be seen smaller openings which were decorated with caskets for ashes and containers; the remaining surfaces of the walls and the vault were divided up in regular manner, and amidst cheerful and varied frames, wreaths and ornamentations, serene and significant figures had been painted in compartments of varying size. The architectural elements were encased in beautiful yellow marble with a tinge of red, bright blue strips of a felicitous chemical composition were in imitation of lapis lazuli and gave the whole unity and harmony, while so to speak satisfying the eye by means of a contrast. All this magnificence and decoration presented itself in pure architectural relationships, and consequently everyone who entered appeared to be elevated, by experiencing for the first time through this integration of art forms what man was and what he might be.

Facing the door one saw on a splendid sarcophagus the marble statue of a worthy and fine man reclining on a couch. He was holding a scroll in front of him and appeared to be gazing upon it with quiet attention. It was so arranged that it was possible to read the words on it with ease. These were: 'Remember to live.'

After removing a faded bunch of flowers, Natalie placed the fresh one in front of the Uncle's likeness; for he himself had been presented in the statue, and Wilhelm believed that he could still recall the features of the old gentleman whom he had seen in the forest on that occasion. 'We spent many an hour here before this room was completed,' Natalie said. 'He had assembled some skilful artists around him in his last years, and his favourite entertainment was to work out the sketches and models for these paintings and to help to decide among them.'

Wilhelm took great pleasure in the objects surrounding him. 'How much life there is in this Room of the Past!' he exclaimed. 'It could just as well be called the room of the present and the future. Thus everything was and thus everything will be! Nothing is transient except the person who is enjoying the scene and viewing it. Here this figure of a mother who is pressing her child to her heart will survive many generations of happy mothers. After centuries perhaps a father will take pleasure in this bearded man who puts aside his seriousness and plays with his son. The bride will sit modestly there for all time and silently wish to be comforted and encouraged; likewise the bridegroom will listen on the threshold to find out whether he may enter.'

Wilhelm's eyes wandered over countless pictures. From the first glad childhood urge to use and practise all his limbs in play to the quiet secluded seriousness of the wise man there could be seen in a beautiful and lively sequence how man possesses no innate inclination and capacity without needing and using them. From the first delicate self-awareness when a girl lingers before lifting up her pitcher from the clear water again and in the meantime takes pleasure in looking at her reflection, to those great occasions when kings and peoples invoke the gods at the altar to be witnesses of their unions, everything was presented in significant and forceful terms.

It was a world, it was a heaven that surrounded the observer at this spot, and apart from the thoughts which those portrayed figures aroused and the emotions which they instilled, something else seemed to be present by which the whole personality felt itself affected. Wilhelm noticed this too, without being able to account for it to himself. 'What is it,' he exclaimed, 'that independently of all significance and free from all the sympathy which human events and destinies cause us to feel, is able to have such a strong and at the same time agreeable effect upon me? It speaks to me from the whole and from each part, without my being able to comprehend the former nor to appropriate the latter to myself particularly! What magic I sense in these surfaces, these lines, these heights and breadths, these masses and colours! What is it that makes these figures so gratifying, even when viewed only perfunctorily and simply as decoration? Yes, I feel that here one could linger and rest, take in everything with one's eyes, find oneself happy and feel and think something that is quite different from what is before one's eyes.'

And certainly, if we could describe how felicitously everything was arranged, how everything was determined on the spot through connection or contrast, through plainness or variety of colour, how everything appeared thus and not differently from the way it should appear and brought about an effect which was as perfect as it was clear, we should be transporting the reader to a place from which he would not wish to leave in haste.

Four large marble candelabras stood in the corners of the room, four smaller ones were in the middle enclosing a very beautifully wrought sarcophagus which from its size could have contained a young person of average build.

Natalie paused by this monument and, placing her hand on it, she said: 'My good uncle had a particular liking for this work from classical antiquity. He often said: "It is not only the first blossoms that fall, which can be preserved up there in those little alcoves, but also fruit that hangs from the branch and for a long time still gives us the greatest hopes while in the meantime a worm is preparing in secret its earlier ripening and its destruction." I'm afraid,' she continued, 'his prophesying was meant for the dear girl who seems to be withdrawing gradually from our care and to be inclining towards this peaceful dwelling-place.'

When they were on the point of leaving, Natalie said: 'There's something else I must draw to your attention. Look at these semi-circular openings on either side up above! Choirs of singers can stand concealed here, and these bronze decorations beneath the ledge serve the purpose of securing the tapestries which are to be displayed at every funeral according to my uncle's directive. He couldn't live without music, especially not without singing, and at the same time had the peculiarity that he did not wish to see the singers. He used to say: "Indeed we have been spoilt too much by the stage, where music is only conducive to our eyes, so to speak, it accompanies movements, not feelings. The figure of the musician always distracts us in oratorios and concerts; true music is for the ear alone; nothing more universal than a beautiful voice can be imagined, and when the limited individual who produces it appears before our eyes, the pure effect of universality is destroyed. I like to see everyone I talk to, for it is an individual person whose figure and character give value, or otherwise, to what is spoken; on the other hand if someone is singing to me, he should be out of sight, his personal appearance should not flatter me nor lead me astray. Here one voice only is speaking to another, not mind to mind, nor a thousand-fold world to the eye, not heaven to man." In a similar way he also wanted to keep orchestras hidden as much as possible in the case of instrumental music, because we are so much distracted and confused by the mechanical movements and the makeshift and always strange gestures of the instrumentalists. For this reason he never used to listen to music except with his eyes shut, in order to concentrate his whole being on the unique, pure pleasure of listening.'

They were about to leave the room when they heard the children running noisily in the corridor, with Felix shouting 'No, me! No, me!'

Mignon was the first to burst in at the open door; she was out of breath and could not bring out a word; Felix, still some distance away, cried: 'Mother Theresa is here!' The children had organized a race, it seemed, in order to bring the news. Mignon lay in Natalie's arms, her heart was beating violently.

'You naughty child,' Natalie said, 'haven't you been told to avoid strenuous exercise? Look how your heart is beating.'

'Let it break!' Mignon said with a deep sigh. 'It's been beating too long any way.'

They had scarcely recovered from this confusion and from this kind of consternation when Theresa entered. She flew to Natalie and embraced her and the good child. Then she turned to Wilhelm, looked at him with her clear eyes and said: 'Now, my friend, how are things? I hope you haven't let yourself be led astray?' He took a step in her direction, she leapt towards him and put her arms round his neck. 'Oh my Theresa!' he exclaimed.

'My friend! My beloved! My husband! Yes, yours for ever!' she called, amid most spirited kisses.

Felix pulled at her skirt, crying: 'Mother Theresa, I'm here as well!' Natalie stood looking on; Mignon suddenly felt for her heart with her left hand, and stretching out her right arm with a violent movement, she collapsed with a shriek at Natalie's feet, dead.

There was great alarm; no movement of heart or pulse could be felt. Wilhelm took her in his arms and carried her in haste upstairs; the dangling body hung over his shoulders. The doctor gave little consolation when he came; he and the young surgeon, whom we know already, made efforts to no purpose. The dear creature could not be brought back to life.

Natalie beckoned to Theresa. The latter took Wilhelm by the hand and led him out of the room. He was silent and without speech, and did not have the heart to look into her eyes. So he was seated by her side on the sofa where he had first encountered Natalie. With great rapidity he thought through a sequence of fateful happenings, or rather he did not think, but allowed what he could not remove to act upon his consciousness. There are moments in life when events move to and fro before us like shuttles and irresistibly complete a piece of weaving which we have more or less spun and laid out ourselves. 'My friend!' Theresa said, 'my beloved!', as she interrupted the silence and took his hand, 'let us support each other at this moment, as we shall perhaps often have to do in similar cases. It is in order to bear such events that people need to face the world as couples. Consider, my friend, and feel that you are not alone, show that you love your Theresa, in the first place by sharing your sorrows with her.' She embraced him and drew him gently to her bosom; he clasped her in his arms and pressed her fiercely to himself. 'In moments of sadness,' he exclaimed, 'the poor child looked for protection and refuge in my uncertain arms; allow the safety of your own heart to stand me in good stead at this terrible hour!' They held each other tightly, he could feel her heart beating against his bosom, but his own mind was bleak and empty; only the images of Mignon and Natalie hovered like shadows within his imagination.

Natalie came in. 'Give us your blessing!' Theresa cried, 'let us be united before you in this sad moment.'—Wilhelm had concealed his face in Theresa's neck; he was fortunate enough to be able to weep. He did not hear Natalie come, he did not see her, his tears merely redoubled at the sound of her voice.— 'I don't want to separate what God is joining together,' Natalie said with a smile, 'but I can't bind you together, and I can't commend the fact that grief and inclination appear to be banishing the memory of my brother from your hearts completely.' At these words Wilhelm released himself from Theresa's arms. 'Where are you going?' the two women asked. 'Let me see the child that I have killed!', he exclaimed. 'The misfortune that we see with our own eyes is smaller than when our imagination violently confronts our minds with the evil; let us go and see the departed angel! Her serene look will tell us that things are well with her!'—As the two women could not restrain the troubled Wilhelm, they followed him, but the good doctor, who was coming towards them with the surgeon, held them back from approaching the deceased girl and said: 'Keep away from this sad object, and permit me to give some permanence to the remains of this strange being, as far as my art enables me. I wish to apply immediately to this dear creature the beautiful art of not only embalming a body but also of preserving in it an appearance of life. As I foresaw her death, I have made all preparations, and with this assistant here I should be successful. Just allow me a few more days' time, and don't ask to see the dear child again until we have brought her into the Room of the Past.'

The young surgeon again had that strange instrument case in his hands. 'Whom did you get it from, I wonder?' Wilhelm asked the doctor. 'I know it very well,' Natalie replied, 'He had it from his father who bound your wounds in the forest that time.'

'Oh, I was not wrong then,' Wilhelm cried out. 'I recognized the ribbon immediately. Let me have it! It brought me for the first time on to the track of my benefactress. What a great deal of happiness and misery take their course while a lifeless object like this survives it all. This ribbon has been in the presence of so much suffering, and its threads still hold. How many people has it already accompanied at their last moments, and its colours have not yet faded! It was present at one of my life's most beautiful moments, when I lay wounded on the ground and your helpful figure appeared before me, when the child with blood-stained hair, whose premature death we are now lamenting, was concerned for my life with most affectionate care.'

The friends did not have much time to talk about this sad event nor to explain to Miss Theresa about the child and the apparent cause of her death; for strangers were announced who, when they showed themselves, were not strange at all. Lothario, Jarno and the Abbé entered. Natalie went up to her brother; a temporary silence befell the others. Theresa said with a smile to Lothario: 'You hardly thought you would find me here, I'm sure; at least it isn't really advisable that we should search each other out at this moment; in the meantime, let me give you my cordial greetings after such a long absence!'

Lothario offered her his hand and rejoined: 'If it should come about that we have to suffer and be resigned, it may well be none the less that good can take place too in the presence of the loved and desired person. I ask for no influence on your decision, and my trust in your heart, your understanding and your purity of mind is still so great that I am glad to place my fate and that of my friend in your hands.'

The conversation at once turned to general, indeed, it may be said, insignificant topics. The company soon broke up in order to go for walks in single couples. Natalie went with Lothario, Theresa with the Abbé, and Wilhelm stayed at the castle with Jarno.

The appearance of the three friends at the moment when Wilhelm's heart was beset by severe grief had irritated and worsened his mood instead of acting as a distraction to him; he was annoyed and suspicious, and could not and would not conceal this when Jarno tackled him about his sullen silence. 'What more is needed?' Wilhelm exclaimed. 'Lothario comes with his assistants, and it would be remarkable if those secret powers of the Tower that are always so busy were not to work on us now and fulfil with and on us some strange purpose or other. From what I know of these holy men, it always seems to be their praiseworthy intention to separate what has been joined together and to join together what has been separated. The sort of tissue that can arise from this may indeed remain an external enigma to our unholy eyes.'

'You are annoyed and bitter,' Jarno said, 'that's all very fine and well. But when you really do get angry, it will be even better.'

'We may be able to manage that,' Wilhelm replied, 'and I am very much afraid that people are taking pleasure this time in trying my innate and acquired patience to the utmost.'

'So in the meantime, until we can see where our stories are leading to,' Jarno said, 'I should like to tell you something about the Tower, which you seem to mistrust so much.'

'It's up to you,' replied Wilhelm, 'if you want to make the venture with a view to my entertainment. My mind is preoccupied by so many things that I don't know whether I can pay due attention to these worthy adventures.'

'I will not let your pleasant mood put me off clarifying you concerning this point,' said Jarno. 'You take me for a clever fellow, and what is more, you should also take me for an honourable one, and again, this time I am carrying out a mission.'— 'I would be glad,' Wilhelm added, 'if you were talking of your own volition and with good intentions in order to enlighten me; and as I can't hear you without mistrust, why should I listen to you?'—'If you have nothing better to do now than to tell fairy-tales, you for your part have surely time to give them some attention; perhaps you will be more inclined to this if I tell you rightaway that everything you saw in the Tower consists in fact only of relics of a youthful venture which at first was a matter of great seriousness for most of the initiated and which now they all only smile at from time to time.'

'So it's only a game as far as these noble signs and words are concerned,' Wilhelm cried out, 'we are led with solemnity to a place which induces reverence in us, we are shown the strangest phenomena, we are given scrolls of magnificent, secret words of wisdom, most of which, it is true, we don't understand, it is revealed to us that up to now we have been apprentices, we are absolved, and we're no wiser than before.'—'Have you not got the parchment close at hand?' asked Jarno, 'there's much that is good in it, for those general sayings are no fabrications; it's true, they will seem empty and obscure to someone who recalls no experience in their context. But give me the so-called Certificate of Apprenticeship, if it's near at hand.'—'Certainly, quite near,' Wilhelm replied, 'an amulet like that should always be worn on one's chest.'—'Well,' Jarno said with a smile, 'who knows whether the contents won't one day find a place in your head and in your heart.'

Jarno glanced inside and ran over the first half with his eyes. 'This part is concerned with the development of the artistic sense, and others may talk of this; the second part is concerned with life, and I'm more at home with that.'

He then began to read passages, speaking in between and adding notes and stories as well. 'Youth is extraordinarily drawn to secrets, ceremonies and big words, and this is often an indication of a certain depth of character. During that period we like to feel stirred and moved in our whole being, even if only in an obscure and vague way. The young man who is intuitively aware of a great deal thinks that he has to find much in a secret, to read much into a secret and to have effect through a secret. The Abbé confirmed a group of young people in these views, partly according to his own principles, and partly from inclination and custom since he had formerly no doubt been in touch with a society that itself may well have accomplished a lot in secret. I was the one who found it most difficult to comply. I was older than others, I had seen things clearly from my childhood days onwards and desired nothing but clarity in all things; I had no other interest except to know the world as it was, and I passed this partiality on to the best of my other companions, and because of this our whole education might have taken a wrong direction; for we began to see only the mistakes of the others and their limitations and to consider ourselves to be excellent characters. The Abbé came to our help and taught us that we should not observe people without becoming interested in their development, and that we are only in a position really to observe and to listen to our own doings. He advised us to retain those first rules of the Society; there was therefore a certain legalistic element carried over into our meetings, one could see no doubt the first quasi-mystical impressions upon the structure of the whole later, as though almost allegorically. It took on the shape of a handicraft that could be elevated to an art. This is where the names of apprentices, assistants and masters came from. We wanted to see with our own eyes and form our own archive of world knowledge; this is how the many confessions originated, which we wrote in part ourselves and in part had written by others, and from which afterwards the Years of Apprenticeship were put together. Not all people are really concerned for their development; many just want a home-made way of finding well-being, recipes for wealth and for every kind of happiness. All those people who did not wish to be set up on their own feet were either delayed or deflected with mystifications and other hocus-pocus. We only absolved in our way those who felt strongly and who clearly acknowledged what their inborn nature was and who had shown themselves sufficiently accomplished to pursue their way with a certain gaiety and lightness.'

'So you have been in much too much of a hurry with me then,' Wilhelm replied, 'for it's exactly since that particular moment that I know least of all what I can, will or ought to do.'—'It was not our fault that we got into this confusion, good fortune may well help us to again; in the meantime just listen: "Someone who is capable of much development will receive enlightenment later about himself and the world. There are only a few who are thoughtful and at the same time capable of action. Thought has an amplifying effect, but is disabling; action brings life, but is limiting."'

'Please don't read to me any more of these strange sayings!' Wilhelm interposed. 'These phrases have made me confused enough already.'—'I will stick to narrative then,' said Jarno, as he half rolled up the scroll and only glanced at it occasionally. 'I myself have been of the least use to the Society and to people; I am a very bad teacher, I find it unbearable to look on when someone is making clumsy efforts, I have to call at once to anyone making mistakes, even if it were a sleepwalker who I could see was in immediate danger of breaking his neck. Because of this I had no end of trouble with the Abbé who maintains that an error can only be cured by erring. We have often argued about you as well; he always used to favour you particularly, and it really means something for his attention to be attracted to you to such a great extent. You must agree with me that I told you the complete truth when I met you.'—'You haven't spared me much,' Wilhelm said, 'and you seem to be faithful to your principles.'—'What is there to be sparing of, after all,' Jarno replied, 'if a young person with various kinds of good potentialities takes a completely wrong direction?' — 'Excuse me,' Wilhelm said, ' you were stern enough in denying me all ability as an actor; I confess to you that although I have wholly given up this art, it is none the less impossible for me to declare that I am completely incompetent in this field.'—'And as far as I am concerned, it is after all clearly decided that anyone who can only be himself on the stage, is no actor. Whoever cannot transform himself into many shapes both in imagination and appearance, does not deserve this name. Thus, for instance, you played Hamlet and some other parts really well, where your character, your appearance and the mood of the moment were of advantage to you. Now that would be good enough for an amateur theatre and for someone who saw no other way ahead for himself.' Looking at the scroll, Jarno continued: ' "We should be on our guard against a talent which we cannot hope to exercise to perfection. We may make as much progress here as we wish, but in the last resort we shall always painfully regret the loss of time and energy spent on such bungling work, once we see clearly the merit of a master in the craft." '

'Don't read anything!' said Wilhelm, 'I ask you in all serious-ness to go on talking, to tell me the story and to make things clear to me! And so it was the Abbé who helped me with *Hamlet* by providing a Ghost?' — 'Yes, for he assured us that it was the only way to cure you, if you could be cured,'—'And that's why he left the veil behind for me and told me to take flight?'—'Yes, he even hoped that after the *Hamlet* performance your whole pleasure would be at an end. Afterwards you would not appear in the theatre again, he maintained; I believed the opposite and was proved right. We argued about it on the very same evening after the performance.'—'And so you have seen me on the stage?' —'Oh, certainly!'—'And who took the part of the Ghost?'—'I don't know, either the Abbé or his twin-brother, but I think it was the latter, he's just a little bit taller.'—'So you have secrets among yourselves as well?'—'Friends can and must have secrets from each other; after all they themselves are no secret from one another.'

'Just to think back to this confusion is confusing to me. Tell me something about the man to whom I owe so much and to whom I have to make so many reproaches.'

'What makes him so estimable to us,' Jarno replied, 'what procures, as it were, his domination over us all is the keen, free view which nature has given to him over all the energies that are indwelling in man and each of which can be developed in its own way. Most people, even the first-rate ones, are only limited; everyone values certain qualities in himself and others; these alone find his favour, and these alone he is willing to work on. The Abbé has quite a different effect, he has understanding of everything and takes pleasure in everything, to recognize and encourage it all. But now I must look into the scroll again!' Jarno continued: '"It is only the totality of human beings that make up mankind, only all energies together comprise the world. From the least, animal-like drive towards craftsmanship to the highest practice of the most spiritual and intellectual art, from the babbling and exulting of children to the most admirable utterances of orators and singers, from the first scufflings of boys to the monstrous procedures by which countries are retained and conquered, from the weakest goodwill and most ephemeral love to the most violent passion and most solemn union, from the clearest awareness of the sensuous presence right up to the faintest intuitions and hopes of the most distant spiritual future, all of this and much more are to be found in man and must be developed; however, not in one person, but in many. Every potentiality is important and must be cultivated. If one person only promotes what is beautiful and the other only what is useful, it is not until both come together that we have a human being. What is useful promotes itself, for it is brought forth by the crowd and cannot be dispensed with; what is beautiful has to be promoted, for few present it and many need it."'

'Stop!' cried Wilhelm, 'I've read all that.'—'Just a few more lines!' Jarno rejoined. 'In this passage I discover the Abbé again, completely: "One force controls another, but none can bring about the development of another; further, in each predisposition alone can be found the force towards self-completion; this is understood by so few people who none the less wish to teach and to be of influence."'—'And I don't understand it either,' Wilhelm interposed.—'You will hear the Abbé speaking about this text often enough still, and so let us just see and grasp in a

truly clear way what there is about *ourselves* and what we can
develop concerning *ourselves*; let us be fair to others, for we only
deserve respect inasmuch as we know how to esteem others.'—
'For God's sake, no more words of wisdom! I feel that they are
a poor remedy for a wounded heart. I would rather you told me
with your terrible precision what it is you expect of me, and
how and in what way you intend to make a sacrifice of me.'—'The
time will come when you will apologize to us for every suspicion
you have had, I can assure you. It is up to you to examine
and to choose, and it's for us to support you. Man is not happy
until his unrestricted striving determines for itself its own limits.
Don't hold on to me, but to the Abbé; don't think of yourself,
but of what is around you. For example, learn to appreciate
Lothario's excellence, how his general view and his activity are
indissolubly linked together, how he is always moving onwards,
and how he extends and expands, and carries everyone along with
him. Wherever he may be, he takes a world along too, his presence
is invigorating and inspiring. On the other hand, consider our
good medicus; his temperament seems to be exactly the opposite.
If the former is effective only with regard to the whole and
to what is distant, the latter directs his clear glance only to
what is nearest, he produces the means to activity rather than
bringing forth and giving life to activity itself; his behaviour
fully resembles good housekeeping, his is a quiet effectiveness,
as he assists everyone in his vicinity; his knowledge is a constant
collecting and distributing, a receiving and imparting on a small
scale. Lothario could possibly destroy in one day something that
the doctor had been building on for years; but perhaps too
Lothario can give to others in one moment the strength to
restore a hundredfold what has been destroyed.'—'It is a sad
business,' said Wilhelm, 'when we are expected to think about
the unmitigated excellences of others at a time when we are
not at one with ourselves; such considerations are no doubt
appropriate to a man in equable mood, not to someone who is
agitated by passion and uncertainty.'—'It is at no time harmful
to observe quietly and rationally, and as we accustom ourselves
to be thinking of the excellences of others, our own good qualities
slip into their place unnoticed and we then gladly give up any
false activities to which imagination may entice us. Liberate your
mind from all suspiciousness and fearfulness, if you can. Here
comes the Abbé, do be friendly to him until you hear even further
how grateful you should be to him. The rogue! There he goes,
between Natalie and Theresa, I should like to bet he's got something in mind. Just as, generally speaking, he has a slight pen-

chant to play the part of fate, so too he can't give up his partiality for arranging a marriage now and again.'

Wilhelm, whose agitated and irritable mood had not been improved by all the sensible and good words of Jarno, found it most indelicate that his friend should mention such a relationship just at that moment, and said, with a smile, though not without bitterness: 'I should think the partiality for arranging marriages should be left to those who are in love with one another.'

Chapter Six

The company had just come together again, and our friends saw themselves compelled to break off the conversation. Shortly afterwards a courier was announced who wished to deliver a letter into Lothario's own hands; the man was brought forward; he looked vigorous and efficient, while his livery was very decorative and in good taste. Wilhelm thought he recognized him, and he was not wrong, it was the same man whom on that former occasion he had sent after Philine and the supposed Mariane and who had not come back again. He was just going to address him when Lothario, who had read the letter, asked in a serious and almost irritated manner: 'What is your master's name?'

'Of all questions that is the one which I can answer least effectively,' the courier modestly replied; 'I hope the letter will give the necessary information; I haven't been given any verbal message.'

'Be that as it may,' Lothario replied with a smile, 'as your master has confidence to write to me in such a foolish manner, he shall be welcome among us.'—'He will not keep you waiting long,' the courier rejoined with a bow, and went off.

'Just listen to this mad, silly message,' said Lothario; 'the unknown person writes as follows: "As of all guests good humour is said to be the most agreeable and as I constantly take it around with me as travelling companion, I am convinced that the visit which I have planned to pay to your Grace and Highness will not be taken amiss, on the contrary I hope to attain the complete approval of the entire elevated family, and on occasion to withdraw again, I remain yours, and so on, Count Snailsfoot."'

'That's a new family,' the Abbé said.

'It may well be a count by temporary appointment,' Jarno put in.

'It's easy to guess the mystery,' Natalie said; 'I bet it's brother Friedrich who has been threatening to visit us ever since Uncle's death.'

'How right you are, beautiful and wise sister!' somebody called from a nearby bush, and at once a pleasant and cheerful young man stepped forward; Wilhelm could hardly hold back a cry. 'What?' he exclaimed, 'is our blonde rogue to turn up here as well?' Friedrich became alert, looked at Wilhelm and said: 'Indeed, I should have been less astonished to find here in my uncle's garden the famous Pyramids which are so firmly fixed in Egypt or the tomb of King Mausolus which, as I have been assured, no longer exists at all, than to find you, my old friend and multiple benefactor. Let me offer you particular and cordial greetings!'

After he had tended greetings and kisses to all around, he again bounded up to Wilhelm and called out: 'Keep him in a good humour for me, this hero, general and dramatic philosopher! When we first met I dressed his hair badly, in fact, I may say that I heckled him with the hackle, though afterwards he saved me from a sound thrashing. He is as magnanimous as Scipio, as generous as Alexander, as well as falling in love now and again, though without hating his rivals. Not that he would heap coals of fire upon his enemies' heads, which, as they say, is supposed to be a poor service to show to anyone, no, he sends good and faithful servants after the friends who are taking his girl away from him so that their feet shan't trip over any stone.'

He continued incessantly in this vein, without anyone being in a position to bring him to a halt, and as nobody could reply to him in the same style, he did most of the talking himself. 'Don't be surprised at my wide reading among sacred and profane scribes; you shall hear how I arrived at this knowledge.' They wanted to learn from him how he was and where he had come from; but because of his ubiquitous moral sayings and old stories he was unable to give a clear explanation.

Natalie said quietly to Theresa: 'His type of merriment hurts me; I would like to wager he doesn't feel at all happy about it.'

As Friedrich found no approval for his jokes among the company, apart from some witticisms which Jarno made in reply to him, he said: 'There is nothing else I can do except to be serious myself with my serious family, and since in such dubious circumstances the full weight of my sins at once falls heavily upon my soul, I will in short come to the decision of making a universal confession, of which, however, you, esteemed ladies and gentlemen, are to hear nothing. This noble friend, who already knows something about my life and doings, shall hear it alone, the more so as he alone has some reason to ask about them. Wouldn't you like to know how and where, who, when and why?' he went on, addressing Wilhelm, 'how about the conjugation of the Greek verb Philéo, Philo, and the derivatives of this most lovely verb?'

With this he took Wilhelm by the arm and led him away, squeezing and kissing him in all sorts of ways.

Friedrich had scarcely got to Wilhelm's room when he noticed a powder-knife by the window with the inscription: 'Remember me.' 'You do look after your valuables well!' he said; 'surely this is Philine's powder-knife which she presented to you that day when I had been pulling at your hair so much. I hope you thought assiduously about the girl whenever you used the knife, and I can assure you that she hasn't forgotten you either, and if I had not long ago banished all traces of jealousy from my heart, I would not be able to look at you without envy.'

'Don't talk any further about this creature!' Wilhelm replied. 'I don't deny that it was a long time before I could get over the impression made by her agreeable presence, but that was all.'

'Shame on you!' Friedrich called, 'who will deny a loved one? And you have loved her as completely as could be wished. Not a day passed without your giving the girl something, and when a German gives a present, he is surely in love. There was nothing else I could do but eliminate her, and in the end then the little red officer did manage this.'

'What? You were the officer whom we met at Philine's and whom she went away with?'

'Yes,' Friedrich added, 'the one you took for Mariane. We had plenty of laughs about the mistake.'

'What cruelty,' Wilhelm exclaimed, 'to leave me in such uncertainty.'

'And as well as that, to take over right away the courier you sent after us!' Friedrich rejoined. 'He's a good fellow and hasn't budged from our side all this time. And I still love the girl as madly as ever. She's bewitched me in quite a special way, so that I almost find myself in a mythological state and every day I'm afraid of being transformed.'

'Just tell me where you got all your display of learning,' Wilhelm asked. 'I've been listening with surprise to the strange habit you've adopted of always making allusions to old stories and fables.'

'It was in the most amusing way that I became learned, indeed, very learned,' Friedrich said. 'Philine was with me, and we rented from a leaseholder the old castle on a knightly estate and lived there as merrily as hobgoblins. There we found a compendious, but choice library, containing a folio Bible, Gottfried's *Chronicle*[1], two volumes of the *Theatrum Europaeum,* the *Acerra Philologica,* Gryphius' writings and some further less important books. Now time did sometimes hang heavily when we had had our fling, we tried to read, and before we knew where we were, time hung even more heavily for us. In the end Philine had the wonderful idea of putting all the books open on a big table, we sat down opposite each other and read to each other, only always sporadically, out of one book and then another. Now that was a real pleasure! We thought we were really in good company where it is considered improper to want to continue with or to discuss in a thorough way any subject for too long; we thought we were in lively company where nobody lets anybody else get a word in edgeways. We passed the time in this way regularly every day, and in consequence we gradually became so learned that we were surprised at it ourselves. We had already discovered that there is nothing new under the sun, our scholarship provided us with evidence for everything. We found all kinds of ways of instructing ourselves. Sometimes we followed an old, defective hour-glass which ran out in a few minutes. One of us quickly turned it round and started reading out of a book, and the sand had hardly finished falling into the lower glass when the other one started to say his piece, and so we really studied in a truly academic manner, except that our hours were shorter and our studies very varied.'

'I can understand this folly when such a merry couple happen to be together,' said Wilhelm; 'but how such a frivolous couple can stay together so long is something I can't understand so easily.'

'That's a matter of good luck and also of bad luck,' Friedrich exclaimed; 'Philine may not be seen anywhere, she doesn't like to see herself, she is expecting. There's nothing in the world more unshapely and ridiculous than she is. Only a short while

1. Johann Ludwig Gottfried was author of *Historische Chronica oder Beschreibung der Geschichte vom Anfang der Welt bis auf das Jahr 1619* ('Historical Chronicle or Description of History from the Beginning of the World to the Year 1619'). *Theatrum Europaeum,* edited by Johann Philipp Abele, appeared in 21 volumes between 1633 and 1718. Peter Lauremberg wrote *Acerra Philologica* ('which is 200 select, useful and memorable stories and discourses compiled from the most famous Greek and Latin writers') (1633). Andreas Gryphius (1616–64), German poet and dramatist. (Tr.)

before I went away, she chanced to come in front of the mirror. "The devil!" she said, turning her face away, "Madame Melina in the flesh! What an awful picture! It really makes you look vile!"'

'I must admit,' Wilhelm interposed with a smile, 'that it is rather funny to think of you two as father and mother.'

'It is a really ridiculous blow that in the end I am supposed to be considered as father. She maintains that this is so, and the time fits in as well. At first I was a bit led astray by the damned visit she paid you after the *Hamlet*.'

'What visit?'

'You surely won't have forgotten all about it in your sleep? The charming and palpable ghost of that night, in case you still don't know, was Philine. It's true, the story was a difficult dowry to take, but if you're not willing to put up with something of the sort, you had better not love at all. Paternity in general depends only on conviction; I am convinced, therefore I am the father. There, you see I know how to use logic in the proper place too. And so long as the child doesn't laugh itself to death as soon as it's born, it may well turn out to be if not a useful, at least an agreeable citizen of the world.'

While the friends were conversing in this cheerful way about frivolous matters, the rest of the company had taken up a serious discussion. Friedrich and Wilhelm had hardly departed when the Abbé led the group without their noticing it into a room overlooking the garden, and when they had sat down he began his discourse.

'We have asserted in general terms that Miss Theresa is not her mother's daughter,' he said; 'we now need to clarify this in some detail. Here is the story, which I am ready to substantiate and prove afterwards in every way.

'Mrs. von — spent the first years of her marriage on very good terms with her husband, only they had the misfortune that the children whose arrival they had hopes of several times were stillborn, and in the third case the doctors forewarned the mother that death might be close, while on a following occasion they prophesied it as completely inevitable. They had to come to a decision, they did not want to dissolve the marriage, they were too comfortable in their household and business arrangements. Mrs. von — tried to find a kind of compensation for the happiness in motherhood that had been denied her through the improvement of her mind, a certain showy style of living and the pleasures of vanity. She was very cheerfully indulgent towards her husband when he was attracted to a woman who looked after all the housekeeping and who had a lovely appearance and a very reliable character. Mrs. von — after a short time aquiesced in an arrangement by which the girl complied with the wishes of Theresa's father, continued looking after the household and showed almost even more assiduity and submission to the lady of the house than she had done before.

'Some time later she announced herself to be pregnant, and the two spouses came to the same sort of idea in this context, though for quite different reasons. Mr. von — wanted to introduce into the house his lover's child as his legitimate one, while Mrs. von —, annoyed because her doctor's indiscretion had caused her position to be known in the neighbourhood, thought that she might regain her regard by means of a substituted child and that by being amenable in this way she might keep an ascendancy in the house which she was afraid of losing in the circumstances. She was more reserved than her husband, she perceived what he wanted and, without meeting him half-way, knew how to facilitate a declaration. She stated her terms and got almost everything she demanded, and so the will was drawn up in which there seemed to be so little provision for the child. The old doctor had died, they turned to a young man who was energetic and clever, he was well rewarded, and he could even seek credit in bringing to light and amending the clumsiness and hastiness of his late colleague. The true mother agreed not unwillingly, the pretence was very well kept up. Theresa was born and made over to a stepmother, while her true mother became a victim of this pretence by venturing out again too soon; she died and left the good man inconsolable.

'Mrs. von — in the meantime had fully achieved her purpose, in the eyes of the world she had a dear child, with whom she made an exaggerated show, at the same time she had been rid of a rival whose position she did after all regard with envious eyes and whose influence, for the future at least, she secretly feared; she overwhelmed the child with affection and was able by means of so lively a sympathy for his loss to draw her husband so to herself in times of intimacy that it may well be said that he yielded to her completely, placed his happiness and that of his child in her hands, and only became master in the house again a short time before his death, and even then to a certain extent only through his grown-up daughter. That is the secret, beautiful Theresa, which your sick father would apparently have been so glad to reveal to you, this is what I wanted to put before you in detail now, just while our young friend, who has become your fiancé through the strangest concatenation of circumstances in the world, is absent from the group. Here are the papers that prove most conclusively what I have maintained. You will at the same time see from them how long I've been on the track of this discovery and how it was that all the same I could not be certain before now; how I did not dare to say anything to my friend about the possibility of happiness, since it would have hurt him deeply if this hope had disappeared a second time. You will understand Lydia's suspiciousness; for I gladly admit that I in no way favoured our friend's liking for this good girl once I could again anticipate his union with Theresa.'

Nobody had anything to say in answer to this strange story. After a few days the women returned the papers without mentioning them further.

There were sufficient ways to hand to occupy the company when they were together; furthermore, the neighbourhood had so many attractions that they enjoyed journeying around it, either alone or in a group, on horseback, by coach or on foot. On one such occasion Jarno fulfilled the mission he had been asked to carry out with regard to Wilhelm and placed the papers before him.

'In these very strange circumstances which I find myself in,' Wilhelm then said, 'I only need to repeat to you what I said straightaway in the beginning in Natalie's presence, and what I said in all sincerity: Lothario and his friends can ask me to perform any kind of renunciation, I herewith place all my claims to Theresa in your hands; procure for me in return my formal release. Oh, my friend, there is no need for great deliberation before I make up my mind! I have felt for some days that Theresa is having to make efforts to preserve even an appearance of the warmth with which she first greeted me here. Her affections are deflected from me, or rather, I have never possessed them.'

'Such situations might be better resolved gradually by waiting quietly,' Jarno rejoined, 'rather than with a lot of talking which always leads to embarrassment and agitation.'

'I should have rather thought that this particular situation would have been likely to be decided upon in the quietest, simplest way,' said Wilhelm. 'I have so often been reproached for hesitation and uncertainty; why, now that I have made up my mind, do other people wish to make the very mistake in their behaviour to me which they blamed me for? Does the outside world take so much trouble to educate us only so that it may make us feel that it cannot itself develop? Indeed, I should be obliged if you would grant me in the near future the satisfaction of having got rid of a mistaken relationship which I became involved in with the purest intentions in the world.'

In spite of this request, a number of days went by during which he heard nothing more about this matter nor did he notice any further change as far as his friends were concerned; in fact, conversation was merely general and on topics that were uninteresting to him.

Chapter Seven

On one occasion Natalie, Jarno and Wilhelm were sitting together, and Natalie began: 'You are in a reflective mood, Jarno, I've been able to notice this about you for some time.'

'That's true,' Jarno replied, 'and I see before me an important enterprise which was prepared among us a long time ago and which must of necessity now be tackled. You already know something about it in general terms, and I am no doubt allowed to talk of it in front of our young friend, since it is expected to be up to him whether he would like to take part in it. You won't see me much longer, for I am on the point of taking a ship to America.'

'To America?' Wilhelm interposed with a smile; 'I wouldn't have expected an adventure of that sort, much less that you would pick me out as your companion.'

'When you know our plan fully,' Jarno replied, 'you will give it a better name and perhaps become attracted by it. Listen to me! You only need to have a slight acquaintance with world affairs to realize that great changes are ahead of us and that there is almost no place where possessions are really secure.'

'I have no clear idea of world affairs,' Wilhelm interposed, 'and have concerned myself with my possessions only very recently. Perhaps I should have done well to put them out of my mind even longer, since I cannot but notice that care for their preservation makes people so self-absorbed.'

'Let me finish!' said Jarno, 'care is befitting to old age, so that youth can be carefree for a time. The balance in human activity can unfortunately only be maintained by opposites. At the present time it is by no means advisable to have possessions at only one locality and to entrust one's money in only one place, and on the other hand it is difficult to supervise what is going on in different locations; we have therefore thought out something different; a society is to radiate out from our old tower and to spread out into all parts of the world, and people will be able to join it from every part of the world. We insure our livelihoods amongst ourselves against the sole eventuality that a political revolution may drive the one or the other of us completely away from his possessions. I am now going to America to make use of the good relationships which our friend established during his stay there. The Abbé intends to go to Russia, and you are to have the choice, if you wish to join us, of either supporting Lothario in Germany or else going with me. I should think you would choose the latter; for it is extremely useful for a young man to undertake a long journey.'

Wilhelm pulled himself together and replied: 'The offer is worthy of full consideration; for after all my motto will soon be: "The further away, the better." I hope you will acquaint me more fully with your plan. It may be my lack of knowledge of the world, but to my mind insuperable difficulties stand in the way of such an association.'

'Most of which will only be removed,' Jarno replied, 'because there are but a few of us up to now, honest, clever and determined people who possess a certain general outlook out of which alone the communal approach can grow.'

Friedrich, who up to now had only been listening, added at that point: 'And if you give me one word of encouragement, I'll come along as well.'

Jarno shook his head.

'Well now, what do you find objectionable about me?' Friedrich continued. 'A a new colony also needs young colonists, and these I can bring along with me immediately; cheerful colonists as well, of that I can assure you. And then I can think of a nice young girl who isn't wanted over here any more, sweet, charming Lydia. Where is the poor child to go with her pain and grief, if she cannot occasionally cast them into the depths of the sea and if she is not taken up by a worthy man? I should have thought, friend of my youth, that as you are in the process of consoling those who have been deserted, you would resolve that each should take his girl under his arm and that we would follow in the wake of the old gentleman.'

This proposition annoyed Wilhelm. He answered with feigned calm: 'I don't even know whether she's free, and as I generally don't seem to be lucky in courtship, I would rather not make such an attempt.'

Natalie then said: 'Brother Friedrich, you think that as you are acting in a frivolous way on your own behalf, your attitude is valid for other people too. Our friend deserves the heart of a woman that would belong to him alone and would not be stirred by alien memories while by his side; a venture of this kind was only to be advised with a most sensible and pure character such as Theresa's.'

'Venture indeed!' cried Friedrich. 'In love everything is a venture. Amid the bushes or at the altar, with embraces or golden rings, to the song of the crickets or to trumpets and drums, it's a venture every time, and chance controls all.'

'I have always observed that our principles are only a supplement to our existence,' Natalie rejoined. 'We are only too glad to drape around our mistakes the garment of a valid law. Just watch out for the path along which you have yet to be led by the beauty who has attracted and is holding you in so forcible a manner.'

'She is in fact on a very good path,' Friedrich replied, 'on the way to saintliness. It's true, it's something of a détour, but all the merrier and more secure; Mary of Magdala went that way too, and who knows how many others. In any case, sister, when love is being talked about it's certainly not for you to intervene. I believe you won't get married before there happens to be a bride missing somewhere and then, in accordance with your usual goodness of heart, you will offer yourself as surrogate to some character or other. So now let us just complete our deal with this seller of souls and come to agreement about our travelling party.'

'You're too late with your proposals,' said Jarno, 'Lydia is taken care of.'

'And in what way?' asked Friedrich.

'I've proposed to her myself,' Jarno replied.

'Old gentleman,' said Friedrich, 'you are making a move there for which, if we regard it as noun, various adjectives could be found and if we regard it as a subject, various predicates.'

'I must honestly admit,' Natalie added, 'that it's a dangerous experiment to claim a girl as one's own at the moment when she is in a state of desperation because she is in love with someone else.'

'I've taken the risk,' Jarno replied, 'subject to a certain condition, she will be mine. And, believe me, there is nothing more estimable in the world than a heart which is capable of love and passion. It doesn't matter whether it has loved in the past or still loves now. The love which is lavished on someone else is almost more appealing to me than the love which I could receive; I can see the strength and force of a loving nature without my own self-love spoiling the pure vision.'

'Have you talked to Lydia in the last few days?' Natalie rejoined.

Jarno nodded with a smile; Natalie shook her head and said, as she stood up: 'I soon shan't know what to make of you any more, but I'm certainly not going to let you confuse me.'

She was about to leave when the Abbé came in with a letter in his hand and said to her: 'Do stay! I've got a proposition here which I would like to have your advice about. The Marchese, the friend of your late uncle, whom we have been expecting for some time, is due to arrive here in the next few days. He writes to me that, as the German language does not come so easily to him as he had thought, he will need a companion who has complete mastery of this language as well as some other qualities; as he wishes to make intellectual rather than political contacts, such an interpreter will be indispensable to him. I can think of no one more suited to this than our young friend. He knows the language, is well informed in many other respects, and it will be a great advantage for him to see Germany in such good company and under such advantageous circumstances. Someone who doesn't know his own country has no standard for judging foreign lands. What do you say, my friends? What do you say, Natalie?'

Nobody raised any objection to the suggestion; Jarno did not seem to see his proposal to go to America as an obstacle, as in any case he would not be setting off straightaway; Natalie did not speak, and Friedrich quoted various proverbs about the value of travelling.

Wilhelm felt so deeply annoyed at this new proposition that he could scarcely conceal it. He saw only too clearly a conspiracy to get rid of him as soon as possible, and worst of all, the intention was made visible quite openly and so wholly without consideration for him. In addition, the suspicions which Lydia had aroused in him, together with all that he had experienced himself, were aroused again in his mind, and the natural manner in which Jarno had expounded everything to him also appeared to him only as a false presentation.

He pulled himself together and answered: 'Indeed, this proposal deserves careful consideration.'

'It might be necessary to come to a quick decision,' the Abbé rejoined.

'I am not prepared for that at the moment,' Wilhelm answered. 'We can wait till the man comes and then see whether we get on together. But one important condition must be accepted in advance, that is, that I may take my Felix with me and have him with me wherever I go.'

'This condition is hardly likely to be granted,' the Abbé replied.

'And I don't see why I should allow anybody to prescribe conditions to me. Nor why, if I should happen to want to see my own country, I need the company of an Italian.'

'Because a young person always needs to make connections,' the Abbé rejoined with a certain impressiveness of manner.

Wilhelm, who was aware that he was not in a condition to restrain himself any longer, as his state was alleviated to some extent only by the presence of Natalie, spoke up in some haste at this point: 'If you give me a little more time to think it over, I imagine it can be quickly decided whether I need to make any more connections, or whether on the other hand heart and reason irresistibly command me to break away from so many kinds of restraints which an eternal and miserable imprisonment threaten me with.'

He spoke thus with feelings that had been very much disturbed. A glance at Natalie reassured him to some extent, as he was impressed all the more deeply at this moment of passion by her appearance and her worth.

'Yes,' he said to himself when he was alone, 'admit to yourself that you love her and you will feel again what it means to be able to love with all one's strength. I loved Mariane like this and had such terrible doubts about her; I loved Philine and had to despise her. I respected Aurelia and could not love her; I admired Theresa, and fatherly love assumed the shape of a fondness for her; and now that all the emotions which ought to make one happy coincide in your heart, you are compelled to take flight! Oh, why must the insuperable desire for possession be associated with these emotions and insights? And why do these particular emotions and convictions, if possession does not take place, completely destroy every other kind of happiness? Shall I in future take pleasure in the sun and the world, in society or any of the things of this world? Will you not always say to yourself: 'Natalie is not there!', and yet unfortunately Natalie will always be present as far as you are concerned. If you close your eyes, she will present herself to you; if you open them, she will hover before all objects like the manifestation which a dazzling image leaves behind in the eye. Was not the quickly passing figure of the Amazon ever present in your imagination, at a former time? And you had only seen her, you did not know her. Now that you know her, that you have been so close to her, and that she has taken so much interest in you, her qualities have been so deeply imprinted on your mind as her picture has ever been imprinted on your senses. Always to be seeking causes anxiety, but it is much more terrible to have found and then to have to leave

what one has found. What else in the world should I now be
asking about further? What else should I be looking around for?
What district or what town holds a treasure comparable to this
one? And am I to travel, only always to be finding what is inferior?
For is life merely like a race-course where you have to turn round
immediately on reaching the furthermost end? And does what is
good and excellent just stand there like a firm, immovable goal
from which one has to leave again with fast horses just as soon as
one thinks one has attained it? Whereas anybody else who seeks
for earthly goods can acquire them at the various points of the
compass or indeed even at the market or the annual fair.

'Come, my dear boy!' he called to his son who had just come
bounding in, 'be and remain everything to me! You were given
to me as replacement for your dearly loved mother, you were to
replace for me the second mother whom I intended for you, and
now you have to fill the even greater gap. Occupy my heart
and my mind with your beauty, your kindness, your thirst for
knowledge and your capabilities!'

The boy was busy with a new musical box, and his father
tried to arrange its mechanism in a more orderly and purposeful
way for him; but at that moment the boy too lost interest in it.
'You are a true member of the human race!' Wilhelm exclaimed;
'Come, my son! Come, my brother! Let us go aimlessly playing
about in the world, as well as we can!'

His decision to leave, to take the child with him, and to find
distraction in what the world had to offer was now his firm
intention. He wrote to Werner, asked him to provide money and
letters of credit, and despatched Friedrich's courier with the
express instruction to come back again soon. However much
annoyed he was at the rest of his friends, his relationship to
Natalie remained unalloyed. He confided his plan to her; she too
assumed that he could and would have to go, and even though her
apparent indifference hurt him, he was completely reassured by
her friendly manner and her presence. She advised him to visit
various towns in order to get to know some of her friends there.
The courier came back, bringing what Wilhelm had asked for,
though Werner did not seem pleased about this new trip. 'My
hopes that you were becoming sensible,' the latter wrote, 'are once
more postponed for a considerable time now. Where are you all
wandering around together this time? And what has happened to
the lady about whose domestic support you led me to make
expectations? What is more, my other friends are not at hand; the
work of the business falls entirely upon the legal adviser and
myself. It is lucky that he is as good with the law as I am with

finance, and that we are both used to being heavily laden. Fare you well! May your extravagances be pardoned, since without them our position in this region could not have been so favourable.'

As far as outward arrangements were concerned, Wilhelm could indeed have made his departure now, but he was held back in his mind still by two obstacles. Once and for all he had been forbidden to see Mignon's body until the obsequies which the Abbé was intending to arrange, and as yet everything was not ready for this solemnity. Furthermore, the doctor had been called away by a strange letter from the country pastor. It concerned the Harpist, about whose fortunes Wilhelm wished to be more closely informed.

In these circumstances he found peace of mind or body neither by day nor at night. When everyone was asleep he went to and fro in the house. The presence of the old, familiar works both attracted and repulsed him. He could neither take up what was surrounding him nor leave it alone, everything reminded him of everything else; he surveyed the whole cycle of his life, only unfortunately it lay broken before him and seemed as if it would not close for all time. These works of art which his father had sold appeared to him to be a symbol, indicating that he too was to be in part excluded from a peaceful and total possession of what is desirable in the world, and in part deprived of this through his own fault or the fault of others. He lost himself to such an extent in these strange and sad observations that he often seemed to himself to be like a ghost and even when he felt and touched the things outside him, he could scarcely resist misgivings as to whether he was properly alive and really there.

Only the intense grief that laid hold of him sometimes, that he would have to leave in such a criminal and yet so essential a manner all that he had found and rediscovered, only his tears restored to him the sense of his identity. It was in vain that he recalled to his mind the happy position in which after all he found himself. 'So everything is worthless,' he exclaimed, 'if man is lacking the one thing he prizes above all else.'

The Abbé announced to the group the advent of the Marchese. 'You have made up your mind indeed, as it seems, to set off alone with your boy,' he said to Wilhelm, 'but do at least meet this man, since he can at all events be useful to you wherever you may encounter each other on your travels.' The Marchese appeared; he was a man not yet advanced in years, a well-made, agreeable Lombardy type. As a young man he had come across the Uncle, who was considerably older than he. in the army and in business affairs; subsequently they had travelled across a large part of Italy together, and the works of art which the Marchese found again here had been brought and procured in his presence and during many happy times that he still remembered well.

Italians in general have a deeper feeling for the high worth of art than people of other nations; everyone who does anything at all wants to be called artist, master and professor, and admits, at least through this craving for titles, that it is not enough simply to seize hold of something when it is handed down nor to acquire some skill or other by practice; he admits rather that everyone should also be capable of thinking and setting up principles about what he does and of making clear to himself and to others the reasons why this or that thing has to be done.

The visitor was moved to discover such beautiful possessions again without their owner and pleased to hear the spirit of his friend speaking from his excellent heirs. They examined the works of art together and took great pleasure in making themselves intelligible to one another. The Marchese and the Abbé took the lead in putting their points of view; Natalie who felt as if she were in her uncle's presence again was very well able to present her opinions and attitudes; Wilhelm had to translate it all into theatre terminology if he wanted to understand anything about it. They had their work cut out to keep Friedrich's jokes within bounds. Jarno was seldom present.

Commenting on the observation that first-rate works of art were so rare in the modern period, the Marchese said: 'It isn't easy to imagine and take in how much circumstances must do for the artist, and then with the greatest genius and most outstanding talent the demands which he has to make of himself are still unending and the diligence necessary for his training is inexpressible. If circumstances do little for him, if he notices that the world is very easily satisfied and merely desires a light, agreeable and comfortable appearance, it would be surprising if ease and self-love did not hold fast to what is mediocre; it would be strange, if he did not prefer to exchange money and acclamation for fashionable wares rather than to choose the right path, which leads him, more or less, to miserable martyrdom. Hence the artists of our time only make offers, but never give. They always want to be stimulating, so that they never bring satisfaction; everything is only hinted at, and nowhere do you find either foundation or realization. But you only need to spend some time quietly in an art-gallery and to observe what works attract the crowd, which are praised and which neglected, in order to take little pleasure in the present and to have little hope for the future.'

'Yes,' added the Abbé, 'and in this way art-lovers and artists educate each other in turn; the art-lover is looking only for general and vague pleasure; the work of art should be agreeable to him in general like a work of nature, and people believe that the organs for the enjoyment of works of art should develop just as much of their own accord as the tongue and the palate, and that judging a work of art is like judging food. They don't understand how different a type of education is required in order to rise to the true appreciation of art. The most difficult thing, I believe, is the kind of seclusion which an individual must bring about in himself if he wants to develop his powers at all; that is why we find so many one-sided civilizations, while each of them presumes to give an unfavourable opinion of the whole.'

'What you are saying now isn't quite clear to me,' Jarno said, who was just joining the group.

'It is also difficult to explain it briefly in a definite manner,' the Abbé replied. 'I will just say this much: as soon as man lays claims to variety of activity or enjoyment, he must at the same time be capable of developing a variety of organs for himself which are, as it were, independent of one another. Whoever wishes to do and enjoy everything with his whole human power, whoever aspires to link up everything outside himself with such a type of enjoyment will only succeed in spending his time in eternally dissatisfied striving. How difficult it is to do what appears so natural, to contemplate a good statue or a fine picture for their own sakes, to listen to a song on account of the song, to admire the actor in the man who is acting, or to take pleasure in a building for the sake of its harmonious structure and its qualities of duration! But now we usually see people treating well defined works of art as if they were soft clay. The shaped marble should at once be re-modelled according to their inclinations, opinions and whims, the building whose walls are firm should be expanded or contracted, a painting should be instructive, a play should be improving, and everything should be capable of becoming everything else. Actually, though, since most people are themselves without form and are unable to give any shape to themselves and their nature, they make efforts to deprive objects of their form in order that everything shall become loose and disconnected matter, which they belong to as well. In the end they reduce everything to the so-called effect, everything is relative, and consequently everything does become relative apart from the nonsense and bad taste which then also dominate totally.'

'I understand you,' Jarno rejoined, 'or rather, I can see how what you say fits in with the principles to which you hold so firmly; but I can't possibly be so specific in dealing with those poor devils, the human race. Certainly I know a sufficient number of them who, when they are confronted by the greatest works of art and nature, at once remember their own most wretched needs, who take their consciences and morality with them to the opera, who don't put aside their loving and hating when viewing a colonnade, and who have first to reduce as far as possible in their imaginations the best and greatest things that can be brought to them from outside, in order to be able to bring them into association, even if only to a limited extent, with their own pitiful personalities.'

Chapter Eight

In the evening the Abbé invited the company to attend Mignon's obsequies. They went to the Room of the Past and found it very strangely illuminated and decorated. Almost from top to bottom the walls were covered with sky-blue tapestries, so that only pedestal and frieze stood out clearly. Large wax-candles were burning on the four candelabras in the corners, and in proportion similarly on the four smaller ones surrounding the central sarcophagus. Near to this four boys were standing, dressed in azure and silver, and seemed to be wafting air with large fans of ostrich feathers towards a figure that was reposing on the sarcophagus. The company sat down, and two invisible choirs began to sing beautifully, asking: 'Whom are you bringing to us in quiet companionship?' The four children answered in pleasing voices: 'We are bringing you a tired playmate; let her rest amongst you until at some future time she is again wakened by the rejoicing of heavenly brothers and sisters.'

CHOIR: First representative of youth in our circle, be welcome, in grief be welcome. May no boy nor girl follow after you. Let only the old approach the silent hall in willingness and composure, and may the dear, dear child rest in solemn company.

BOYS: Alas, how reluctantly we brought her here! Alas, and she is to remain here. Let us stay too, let us weep, weep at the child's coffin.

CHOIR: But look at the powerful wings! Look at the light, pure
    robe. How the golden wrap gleams from her head! See her
    beautiful, dignified repose.
BOYS: Alas! The wings do not raise her up; the dress no longer
    flutters in light-hearted play; when we crowned her head with
    roses, she looked at us in gracious and friendly manner.
CHOIR: Look upward with the eyes of the spirit. May the formative
    power live within you which raises on high what is most
    beautiful and most elevated, carrying life above the stars.
BOYS: But alas, we miss her here, she does not walk in the
    gardens any longer nor collect meadow flowers. Let us weep,
    we are leaving her here. Let us weep and remain with her!
CHOIR: Children, turn back to life. May your tears be dried
    by the fresh air that plays around the winding stream. Take
    flight from night. Day, happiness and continuance are the lot
    of the living.
BOYS: Come, we are turning back to life. May the day give us
    work and happiness until evening brings us peace and nocturnal
    sleep refreshes us.
CHOIR: Children, hurry on into life! May love encounter you in
    the pure garment of beauty with heavenly glance and the
    wreath of immortality.

The boys were already far off, the Abbé rose from his seat and
stepped behind the coffin. 'It is the decree of the man who prepared this quiet resting-place,' he said, 'that each new arrival
should be received with solemnity. The first person we brought
here after himself, the builder of this house and founder of this
abode, was a younger stranger, and so this little room already contains
two very different sacrifices to the severe, arbitrary and inex-
orable goddess of death. We enter life according to definite laws,
the days are numbered which make us mature to look upon the
light, but there is no law for the duration of life. The feeblest
life-thread can draw out to an unexpected length, and the scissors
of the goddess of fate who seems to delight in contradictions
can forcibly cut off the strongest. We know of little to say about
the child whom we are burying here. Where she came from is
still unknown; we do not know her parents and we can only
estimate her age. Her deeply reserved heart scarcely allowed us to
guess her innermost concerns; nothing was clear about her,
nothing revealed, except her love for the man who saved her
from the hands of a barbarian. This tender affection and lively
gratitude seemed to be the flame which consumed the oil of her
life; the doctor's skill could not preserve her noble life nor could

the most caring friendship prolong it. But if art could not hold back the departing spirit of life, it has made use of all its means to preserve the body and to withdraw it from transience. A balsam mass has suffused all the veins and now gives colour in place of blood to the cheeks that turned pale so soon. Step nearer, my friends, and see the miracle of art and care!'

He lifted the veil, and the child was lying in her angel garment as if asleep in a very pleasing position. Everyone stepped up and admired this replica of life. Only Wilhelm remained seated in his chair, unable to remain composed; what he felt, he was not allowed to think, and every thought seemed to wish to destroy his feeling.

For the sake of the Marchese the speech had been made in French. He came up with the others and examined the figure attentively. The Abbé continued: 'This loving heart, which was so withdrawn from human beings, was constantly turned to her God with holy trust. Humility, indeed a tendency towards outward self-abasement, seemed inborn in her. She held zealously to the Catholic religion in which she had been born and brought up. She often expressed the quiet wish to rest on consecrated ground, and following the customs of the Church we have consecrated this marble receptacle and the small amount of earth which has been concealed in her pillow. With what passion did she in her final moments kiss the picture of the Crucified One which is very gracefully reproduced with many hundred points on her delicate arms!' While saying this, he exposed her right arm, and a crucifix accompanied by various letters and signs could be seen, bluish upon the white skin.

The Marchese examined this new phenomenon at close quarters. 'Oh, God!' he cried out, as he raised himself up and lifted his hands towards heaven, 'Poor child! Unhappy niece! Do I find you again here? What a grievous joy it is to find you again here, you whose loss we had accepted so long ago, this dear, good body which for a long time we thought had become a prey of the fishes, dead, it is true, but preserved! I am attending your funeral which is so splendid in its external form and is becoming even more splendid because of the good people who are accompanying you to your resting-place. And when I can speak again,' he said with broken voice, 'I shall thank them.'

Tears prevented him from saying any more. By the pressure of a spring the Abbé caused the body to be lowered into the depths of the marble. Four young men, dressed like the boys earlier, stepped forward behind the tapestries, lifted the heavy and beautifully decorated lid on to the coffin and at once began their singing.

THE YOUNG MEN: The treasure, beautiful image of the past, is now well secured. It rests unconsumed here in the marble; it lives on and continues to have influence in your hearts also. Go back, go back into life. Take sacred earnestness out with you, for earnestness, sacred earnestness, alone turns life into eternity.

The invisible choir joined in with the final words, but none of the company heard the fortifying phrases, each was too much occupied with the strange disclosures and with his own emotions. The Abbé and Natalie led the Marchese, Wilhelm, Theresa and Lothario out, and it was not until the singing had completely ceased to sound that they were once more beset with full force by grief, observations, thoughts and curiosity, and they longed to return again to that element.

Chapter Nine

The Marchese avoided talking about the matter, but had long, secret discussions with the Abbé. When they were together as a group he often asked for music; this request was gladly complied with as everyone was glad to be excused from conversation. They continued to live like this for some time, until it was noticed that the Marchese was making preparations to leave. One day he said to Wilhelm: 'I do not wish to disturb the remains of the dear child; let her remain behind at the place where she loved and suffered, but her friends must promise to visit me in her home-country, at the place where the poor creature was born and brought up; they must see the columns and statues of which she still retained an obscure idea.

'I will take you to the bays where she so much used to like gathering pebbles. My dear young man, you will not shrink from the gratitude of a family which owes you so much. I am leaving tomorrow. I have confided the whole story to the Abbé, he will tell it again to you; he could forgive me when my grief interrupted me, and as a disinterested person he will narrate the events more coherently. If you still wish to follow me on my journey through Germany, as the Abbé has suggested, you are welcome. Don't leave your boy behind; at every small inconvenience that he causes us we will recall again your care for my poor niece.'

That very evening they were surprised by the arrival of the Countess. Wilhelm trembled in all his limbs when she entered, and although she had been prepared, she kept near her sister who soon offered her a chair. How strangely simple her clothing was, and how changed her appearance! Wilhelm scarcely ventured to look at her; she greeted him in a friendly way, and a few general remarks were not able to conceal her attitude and feelings. The Marchese had gone to bed early, and the company did not have as yet any wish to break up; the Abbé produced a manuscript. 'I have just put down on paper the strange story, exactly as it was confided to me,' he said. 'The last occasion when we should save pen and ink, is the writing up of the particular circumstances of noteworthy events.' The Countess was informed what the subject was, and the Abbé read his account:

'For all that I have seen a lot of the world (the Marchese said), I must always consider my father to be one of the most unusual men. His character was noble and honest, his ideas extensive, and one may say, great; he was severe towards himself; in all his plans could be found a stern sequence, while all his actions were characterized by uninterrupted, measured steps. However advantageous it was, therefore, from one point of view to have to do with him and to negotiate in business, it was all the more difficult for him to find his way in the world precisely because of these qualities, since he required the state, his neighbours, children and servants to observe all the laws which he had laid upon himself. His most moderate requests were exaggerated by his sternness, and he could never find enjoyment because nothing came to pass in the way he had anticipated. At the moment when he was building a palace, laying out a garden, acquiring a large new estate in the most beautiful situation, I have seen him inwardly gripped with extreme rage and convinced that fate had condemned him to be abstemious and to be patient. Outwardly he exhibited the greatest dignity; if he joked, he only showed the superiority of his intellect; he found it unbearable to be reproved, and only on one occasion in my life have I known him to be completely disconcerted, when he heard one of his projects talked about as something ridiculous. It was precisely in this spirit that he had made arrangements concerning his children and his fortune. My eldest brother was brought up to be a man who had hopes of having great estates in the future; I was to take holy orders, and the youngest brother was to become a soldier. I was lively, fiery, active, quick, and suited to all physical accomplishments. My youngest brother seemed more inclined towards a kind of ecstatic quietness and to be devoted to learning, music and literature. Only after the most vigorous struggle and after being completely convinced of the impossibility of the situation did our father give way, albeit reluctantly, and although he saw that the two of us were happy, he could not be reconciled to it none the less and he was sure that nothing good would come of it. The older he became, the more cut off he felt from all society. Finally he lived almost completely alone. His only company was an old friend who had served under the Germans, had lost his wife in the course of a campaign and had brought with him a daughter who was about ten years old. This man bought a pleasant estate in the neighbourhood, and used to see my father on certain days and times in the week, when he also often brought his daughter with him. He never contradicted my father who in the end became completely used to him and tolerated him as the only bearable companion he could find. After our father's death we noticed indeed that this man had been very well provided for by our parent and had not been wasting his time; he extended his estates, and his daughter could look forward to a handsome dowry. The girl grew up and was particularly beautiful; my older brother often joked with me, saying that I ought to woo her.

'In the meantime our brother Augustine had spent some years in the monastery in the strangest state of mind; he yielded completely to the enjoyment of a holy enthusiasm, to those half spiritual, half physical feelings which, if they raised him up to the seventh heaven for a time, soon afterwards caused him to sink into an abyss of weakness and into a state of empty wretchedness. During my father's lifetime it was no use thinking of any change, and what was there that should have been desired or suggested? After our father's death he visited us regularly; his condition, which distressed us at first, gradually became much more bearable, for reason had prevailed. But the more surely reason promised his complete contentment and healing by means of the pure way of nature, the more vigorously he demanded that we should liberate him from his vows; he intimated that his aspirations were directed towards Sperata, our neighbour.

'My elder brother had suffered too much from our father's hardness for him to be able to remain unmoved at the condition of the youngest brother. We talked with our family confessor, an old and estimable man, revealed to him our brother's double intention and requested him to initiate and advance the matter. He hesitated, which was unusual for him, and when finally our brother pressed us and we recommended the business to the priest in more urgent terms, he had to make up his mind to reveal the strange story to us.

'Sperata was our sister, being indeed daughter of both our father and mother; inclination and sensuality had overcome the man again in those later years when the rights of spouses appear to have been extinguished; shortly before, people had made fun of a similar case in the neighbourhood, and in order not to expose himself likewise to ridicule, my father determined to keep secret this late, lawful fruit of love with the same care with which in other instances people usually conceal the earlier, chance fruits of inclination. Our mother was confined in secret, the child was taken into the country, and the old friend of the family, who was the only person to know about the secret apart from the father confessor, easily let himself be persuaded to proclaim her as his daughter. The father confessor had only stipulated that he should be allowed to reveal the secret in an extreme emergency. The father had died, the tender girl lived under the supervision of an old woman; we knew that singing and music had already procured our brother's introduction to her, and as he repeatedly requested us to untie his old bonds so that the new union could be joined, it was necessary to inform him as soon as possible of the danger in which he stood.

'He looked at us with wild, contemptuous glances. "Keep your unlikely fairy-tales for children and credulous fools!" he exclaimed. "You won't tear Sperata from my heart, she is mine. Take back at once your terrible ghost which would only frighten me in vain. Sperata is not my sister, she is my wife!"—He described to us with delight how the lovely girl had led him from a state of unnatural separation from people into true life, how their two temperaments, like their two voices, harmonized together, and how he blessed all his sufferings and errors because they had kept him apart from all women up to then, and because now he could devote himself completely to the most delightful girl. We are horrified at this discovery and distressed at his position, we did not know what to do, he assured us with vehemence that Sperata was carrying his child in her womb. Our father confessor did all his duty prompted him to, but this only made bad worse. The relationships between nature and religion, ethical rights and civil laws were fought out by my brother in the most impetuous way. Nothing seemed sacred to him except his relationship with Sperata, nothing seemed worthy of respect to him other than the name father and wife. "These alone are according to nature," he exclaimed, "everything else is fancy and opinion. Were there not noble peoples who permitted marriage with a sister? Don't talk about your gods," he called out, "you never use their names except when you want to delude us, to lead us away from nature's path and to misrepresent through shameful compulsion the noblest instincts as crimes. You compel the victims whom you bury alive to the greatest confusion of the mind and to the most shameful abuse of the body.

'"I may speak, for I have suffered as no one else has, from the highest, sweetest fulfilment of ecstasy to the terrible desert wastes of impotence, emptiness, destruction and despair, from the highest intimations of supernatural beings to the most complete disbelief, disbelief in myself. I have drunk up all these fearful dregs from the cup whose rim is so enticing, and my whole being was poisoned to its core. Now that kindly nature has healed me again by means of her greatest gifts, through love, now that in the embrace of a wonderful girl I feel once more that I am, that she is, that we are one, and that from this living union a third being is to be formed and to smile at us, now you reveal the flames of your hells and purgatories which can scorch only a sick imagination and contrast them with the true, living, indestructible enjoyment of pure love! Come to us beneath those cypresses that raise their grave tops towards heaven, visit us by those espaliers where lemons and oranges flourish, where the delicate myrtle offers us her tender flowers, and then dare to terrify us with your dismal grey meshes that have been spun by human hands!"

'In this way he insisted for a long time on an obstinate disbelief of our story, and finally when we had assured him of its truth and the father confessor himself affirmed it to him, he none the less did not let himself be confused by it, indeed he called out: "Do not ask the echoing of your cloisters nor your mouldering parchment nor your intricate fancies and ordinances, ask nature and your heart, they will teach you what you need to feel dread of, this will point out to you with the strictest finger what it is they pronounce their curse on eternally and irrevocably. Look at the lilies: do not husband and wife originate from *one* stem? Are not both bound by the flower that gave them both birth, and is not the lily the image of innocence, and is not its union of brother and sister fruitful? When nature expresses abhorrence, she does so out loud; the creature that is not intended to be cannot come into existence, the creature that lives falsely is destroyed early. Infertility, a wretched existence and premature decay are her fruits, the symptoms of her severity. She only punishes by direct consequences. There! Look around you and it will be apparent to you what is forbidden and accursed. In the quiet of the monastery and in the noise of the world a thousand actions are hallowed and respected upon which nature's curse lies. She looks down with sad eyes upon easy indolence as much as on overstrained work, upon recklessness and super-abundance as much as on want and need, she calls to moderation, her circumstances are all true and her efforts all peaceful. He who has suffered as I have has the right to be free. Sperata is mine; only death shall take her from me. How I can keep her and how I can become happy is your responsibility! Now I am going straight to her in order not to be separated from her again.''

'He wanted to go to the ship in order to travel across to her; we restrained him and asked him not to take any step that might have the most terrible consequences. He should consider that he did not live in the free world of his thoughts and imaginings, but in a situation whose rules and circumstances had taken on the unassailability of a law of nature. We had to promise the father confessor that we would not let our brother out of our sight and certainly not let him leave the castle; after that he left and promised to return in a few days. What we had antici-pated, occurred; reason had made our brother strong, but his heart was tender; earlier religious impressions asserted themselves, and the most dreadful doubts took hold of him. He spent two fearful days and nights; the father confessor came to his assistance again, but in vain! Reason, which was uncommitted and free, exonerated him; his feelings, his religion, and all habitual ideas declared him to be a criminal.

'One morning we found his room empty, there was a note on the table in which he explained to us that as we were keeping him prisoner by force, he was justified in seeking his freedom; he was taking flight and going to Sperata, he was hoping to escape with her, he would be ready for anything if an attempt was made to separate them.

'We were not a little alarmed, but the father confessor begged us to be calm. Our poor brother had been supervised closely; the sailors, instead of taking him across, took him to his monas-tery. Wearied by forty hours without sleep, he fell asleep as soon as the boat was rocking him in the moonlight, and did not awaken until he found himself in the hands of his ecclesiastical brethren; he did not come to himself until he heard the monastery door slam behind him.

'Painfully moved by our brother's fate, we made the most vigorous remonstrations to our father confessor; but this revered man could soon persuade us with a surgeon's reasoning, that our pity for the poor sick man would kill him. He told us that he was not acting on his own impulse, but on the orders of the Bishop and the great council. The intention was to avoid any public disclosure and to conceal the tragic case under the veil of secret ecclesiastical discipline, Sperata was to be spared and not to learn that her beloved was also her brother. She was recommended to the care of a priest to whom she had earlier confided her condition. It was possible to conceal her pregnancy and confinement. As a mother she was very happily absorbed in the little one. Like most of our womenfolk she could neither read nor write; she therefore gave the priest messages that he should pass on to her beloved. The priest believed himself obliged to practise pious deception on the nursing mother, he brought her news of our brother whom he never saw, admonished her to keep quiet in his name, and begged her to look after herself and the child and to trust God as far as the future was concerned.

'By nature Sperata was inclined to be religious. Her condition and her solitude gave emphasis to this trait, the priest encouraged it in order to prepare her gradually for an eternal separation. No sooner had the child been weaned, no sooner did he believe that her body was strong enough to bear the most fearful torments of mind, than he began to paint the transgression to her in terrible colours, the transgression of having yielded to a priest, which he treated as a kind of sin against nature, as a form of incest. For he had the strange idea of making her remorse comparable to the remorse she would have felt if she had learnt about the true nature of her misdemeanour. In this way he filled her mind with so much distress and worry, he exalted the idea of the Church and its Head so much before her, he showed her the terrible consequences as regards the salvation of all souls if one were to give way in such cases and indeed even to reward those who were culpable by providing a legal union; he showed her how salutary it would be to expiate such a failing in this world and consequently to win the crown of glory at some future time, that in the end, like a poor sinner, she gladly offered her neck to the axe and fervently implored that she should be separated for ever from her brother. After obtaining so much from her, she was allowed the freedom, though under some supervision, to be sometimes at her home and sometimes in the convent, according to what she thought right.

'Her child grew and soon showed a singular nature. She could walk very early and could move with complete adroitness, she soon sang very agreeably and learned to play the zither by herself, as it were. It was only in words that she could not express herself, and the impediment seemed to be in her ability to think rather than in her vocal organs. The poor mother meanwhile suffered sadly in her relationship to the child; the priest's treatment had so confused her mind that she experienced the strangest conditions, though without being mad. Her offence seemed to her to be becoming ever more terrible and culpable; the priest's often repeated analogy of incest had imprinted itself so deeply upon her that she felt as great a repugnance as if the relationship itself had been known to her. The father confessor was not a little pleased at the clever device with which he was breaking the heart of an unhappy creature. It was distressing to see how mother-love which had been prepared for such heartfelt happiness at the child's existence was wrestling with the dreadful thought that this child should not be there. At times these two feelings were in conflict, at times revulsion dominated over love.

'It was quite a time since the child had been taken from Sperata and given into the care of good people down by the lakeside, and with the increased freedom which the child now had, her particular pleasure in climbing soon emerged. It was a natural urge on her part to climb the highest peaks, to run off on the sides of ships and to imitate the strangest tricks of the tightrope-walkers who appeared in the locality from time to time.

'So that she might do all these things more easily, she loved to change clothes with the boys, and although her foster-parents thought this most indecent and inadmissible, we were indulgent to her as far as possible. Her leaping and the strange paths she took frequently led her far afield; she got lost, was missing, and always came back again. Mostly, when she returned, she sat down beneath the columns of the portals of a country house in the neighbourhood; people no longer went to look for her, she was expected. She seemed to be resting on the steps there, then she would run into the great hall and look at the statues, and if she were not specially detained, she would hurry home.

'Finally, however, our hopes were disappointed and our leniency punished. The child was missing, her hat was found floating in the water, not far from the spot where a mountain torrent rushed down into the lake. It was assumed that she had had an accident while climbing among the rocks; for all the investigations that were made, the body was not to be found.

'Sperata soon learned about her child's death from the careless talk of her woman companions; she seemed calm and serene, and made it clear that she was happy that God had taken the poor creature to Himself and had thus prevented her from suffering or initiating a greater misfortune.

'With this happening, there was talk about all the fairy-tales which people are accustomed to tell about our waters. It was said that the lake had to have an innocent child every year; that it would not tolerate any dead body and would throw it ashore sooner or later, indeed, even the last little bone would have to come out again, even if it had sunk to the bottom. The story was told of the inconsolable mother whose child had been drowned in the lake and who pleaded to God and His saints to allow her to have at least the bones for burial; the next storm was said to have brought the skull to the shore, the storm after that to have brought the torso, and after it had all been collected together, she had taken all the bones in a cloth to the church, but, wonder of wonders, when she went into the church the package had grown heavier and heavier, and finally when she had placed it on the altar steps the child had started to cry, and to everyone's surprise had made its way out of the cloth; all that was missing was a small bone of the little finger of the right hand, and this the mother subsequently looked for with care and did find; it was then preserved as a memorial with other relics in the church.

'These stories made a great impression on the poor mother; her imagination sustained a new impetus and encouraged the feeling in her heart. She assumed that the child had now made expiation for herself and her parents, that the malediction and punishment which had lain upon her hitherto were now completely removed; that it was only a matter of finding the child's remains and taking them to Rome, and then the child would stand again before all the people, with its beautiful, fresh skin, on the steps of the high altar of St. Peter's. With her own eyes the child would look upon her father and mother again, and the Pope, convinced of the consent of God and His saints, would forgive the parents their sin, absolve them and unite them amid the loud acclaim of the people.

'Now her eyes and her attention were always directed to the lake and the shore. When the waves broke at night in the moonlight, she believed that every bright edge of foam would be bringing forth her child; someone had to rush down apparently in order to pick the child up by the shore.

'During the day-time too she was tirelessly present at the places where the pebbly beach ran flat into the water; she collected all the bones she found into a little basket. Nobody was allowed to tell her that they were animals' bones; she buried the big ones and kept the little ones. She continued constantly in this occupation. The priest, who had been the cause of her condition through the unceasing exercise of his duty, now also took up her cause with all his energies. Through his influence she was considered in the neighbourhood to be mentally transported, not mad; people stood with folded hands when she went by, and the children kissed her hand.

'Her old friend and companion was only absolved by the father confessor from the guilt that she might have had in connection with the unhappy union of the two persons on condition that she should accompany the unfortunate woman with unceasing loyalty for the rest of her life, and she did in fact carry out her duties to the end with admirable patience and conscientiousness.

'In the meantime we had not forgotten our brother; neither the doctors nor the ecclesiastical authority of his monastery were willing to allow us to appear before him; only in order to convince us that things were going well with him in his way, we could spy on him in the garden, in the cloisters, indeed through a window by the ceiling of his room.

'After many a terrible and extraordinary episode, which I will pass over, he achieved a strange state of peace of mind and restlessness of body. He almost never sat down, except when he took up his harp and played on it, when for the most part he accompanied his playing with singing. Moreover he was always moving about, and was extremely tractable and docile in all things; for all his passions seemed to have been dissolved into one single fear, the fear of death. It was possible to make him do anything in the world if you threatened him with a dangerous illness or with death.

'Apart from this peculiarity, that he walked tirelessly back and forth in the monastery and that he gave people clearly to understand that it would be even better to be wandering across mountains and valleys in this way, he also spoke of an apparition that frequently terrified him. He asserted in fact that if he woke up at any time of the night, a beautiful boy would be standing at the foot of his bed, threatening him with a bare knife. He was put into another room, but he maintained that the boy was lying in wait for him there as well, and eventually even in other parts of the monastery. His pacing to and fro became more restless, indeed people remembered afterwards that at this time he would stand at the window and look across the lake more frequently than usual.

'Our poor sister meanwhile seemed to be becoming gradually more worn out by the one single thought and the limited form of occupation, and our doctor suggested mixing the bones of a child's skeleton little by little with her other bones in order to increase her hope by these means. It was a dubious experiment, but at least so much seemed to be gained by it that it was possible to deflect her from her eternal searching and to give her the hope of a journey to Rome.

'This took place, and her companion imperceptibly exchanged the remains that had been entrusted with her with those that had been found, and the poor sick woman became filled with an incredible rapture when the parts could be gradually fitted together and those which were still missing could be designated. With great care she had fastened every part where it belonged with thread and ribbons; she had filled the intermediate spaces with silk and embroidery, in the style in which people are accustomed to revere the bodies of saints.

'In this way the limbs had been collected, all that was missing consisted of some parts of the extremities. One morning when she was still asleep and the doctor had come to inquire after her, the old woman removed the venerated remains from the casket which was in the bedroom in order to show him how the invalid was spending her time. Shortly after this the latter could be heard leaping out of bed; she lifted up the cloth and found the casket empty. She went down on her knees; the others came and heard her joyful, ardent prayers. "Yes, it is true!" she exclaimed, "it was no dream, it is real! Rejoice with me, my friends! I have seen the dear, lovely creature again alive. She stood up and threw aside the veil, her radiance lit up the room, her beauty was transfigured, she could not step on the ground although she wanted to. She was gently lifted up and could not even give me her hand. Then she called me to her and showed me the way I should go. I shall follow her, and follow her soon, I can feel it, and my heart is so light. My anxieties have gone, and just the sight of my resurrected dear one has given me a foretaste of heavenly joy."

'From this time on her entire consciousness was concerned with the most cheerful prospects, she no longer directed her attention to any earthly object, she took little food, and her spirit gradually became disengaged from the bonds of the body. What is more, at the end she was found to be unusually pale and without feeling; she did not open her eyes again, she was what we call dead.

'Talk of her vision had soon spread among people, and the revered reputation which she had enjoyed in her lifetime quickly changed after her death into the concept that she would immediately have to be esteemed as blessed, indeed as holy.

'When arrangements were made to bury her, many people pressed round with incredible impetuosity; they wanted to touch her hand, or at least her dress. In this passionate exaltation a number of sick people did not feel the pains which usually tormented them; they considered themselves cured and proclaimed it, they praised God and His new saint. The church officials were compelled to place the body in a chapel, the people demanded the opportunity to perform their acts of worship, the pressure of the crowds was unbelievable; those living in the mountain areas, who in any case are inclined to strong religious feelings, came along from their valleys; the devotion, the miracles, and the worshipping increased daily. The episcopal regulations, which were intended to limit any such new practice and gradually to crush it, could not be carried out; at every act of resistance the people became vehement and ready to have resort to violence against any unbeliever. "Did not Saint Borromeo also walk among our forefathers? Did not his mother experience the rapture of his beatification? Was not the intention of that great effigy on the rocks by Arona to present to us his spiritual greatness in sensuous form? Are not his descendants still among us? And has not God consented to go on renewing his miracles in the midst of a believing people?"

'When after some days the body showed no signs of corruption but rather became whiter and, as it were, translucent, peoples' trust grew more and more, and there appeared among the populace various cures which even an attentive observer could not explain and which also could not exactly be considered to be deception. The whole district was in a ferment, and if anybody did not come to see for himself, for a time at least there was nothing else he could hear talk of.

'The monastery where my brother was resounded with talk of these miracles as much as the rest of the neighbourhood, and people were all the more incautious about talking of it in his presence as he was normally indifferent to everything and nobody knew about his circumstances. But this time he seemed to have listened with much attention; he carried out his escape with such cunning that no one could understand how he got out of the monastery. It was learnt afterwards that he had crossed with a party of pilgrims and that he had asked the sailors, who otherwise did not observe anything unusual about him, only that they should be particularly careful not to let the boat capsize. It was far into the night when he came to the chapel where his unhappy beloved was at rest after her suffering; there were only a few pious people kneeling in the corners, her old friend was sitting at her head, he stepped up and greeted her, and asked how her mistress was. "You can see," she replied, not without embarrassment. He only looked at the corpse from the side. After some hesitation he took hold of her hand. Startled by the coldness, he at once let it go again, he looked round uneasily and said to the old woman: "I can't stay with her now, I've still got a very long way to go, but I intend to be back again in good time; tell her that when she wakes up!"

'This is how he went off, we were not informed about this happening until later, investigations were made as to where he could have got to, but in vain! It's incomprehensible how he could have made his way across mountains and valleys. Finally, after a long time, we found a trace of him again in the Grisons, only too late, and it was soon lost. We assumed that he had gone to Germany, only what faint traces he left were completely obliterated by the war.'

Chapter Ten

The Abbé stopped reading, and nobody had been listening without tears. The Countess did not remove her handkerchief from her eyes; in the end she got up and left the room with Natalie. The others were silent, and the Abbé said: 'The question now arises as to whether we should let the good Marchese depart without revealing our secret to him. For who indeed can doubt for a moment that Augustine and our Harpist are one and the same person? We must consider what is to be done, both for the sake of the unfortunate man as well as for the family. My advice would be not to be in too much of a hurry, and to wait for what news may be brought to us by the Doctor, whom we are just expecting back from there.'

Everyone was of the same opinion, and the Abbé continued: 'Another question, which can perhaps be dealt with more quickly, arises at the same time. The Marchese has been extremely moved by the hospitality that his poor niece found among us, in particular on the part of our young friend. I have had to tell him the story in detail, in fact repeatedly, and he has expressed his most intense gratitude. "The young man declined to travel with me before he knew what the relationship between us is. As far as he is concerned, I am no longer a stranger whose manner and mood he might perhaps not be sure of; I am his ally, if you like, his relative, and as his boy, whom he did not want to leave behind, was the obstacle which in the first place kept him back from accompanying me, do let this child now become the beautiful bond that links us all the more firmly to one another. As well as the obligation which I now have, I hope he will be of further service to me during the journey, I hope he will come back with me, my elder brother will receive him with pleasure, and I hope he will not disdain the inheritance of his fosterchild; for according to a secret agreement between our father and his friend, the wealth which he had bestowed on his daughter has come back to us, and we certainly don't want to withhold from our niece's benefactor what he has merited."'

Theresa took Wilhelm's hand and said, 'Once more we are experiencing a lovely example of how unselfish beneficence brings in interest of the highest and finest kind. Follow this unusual call, and in making yourself doubly useful to the Marchese, hasten towards a beautiful land which has attracted your imagination and your heart on more than one occasion.'

'I will yield completely to my friends and their guidance,' Wilhelm said; 'it is futile to strive in this world for one's own aims. I have to let go what I wished to hold fast, and an unmerited kindness is being thrust upon me.'

After pressing Theresa's hand Wilhelm withdrew his own. 'I leave it to you completely,' he said to the Abbé, 'to decide what you like about me; so long as I don't have to be parted from my Felix, I am ready to go anywhere and to undertake anything that is considered right.'

Following this declaration, the Abbé at once outlined his plan: they should let the Marchese set off, Wilhelm was to wait for the Doctor's news, and then, after they had considered what needed doing, Wilhelm could follow with Felix. So he also indicated to the Marchese that the young friends' preparations for the journey should not prevent the Marchese in the meantime from examining the sights of the city. The latter departed, not without repeated and warm assurances of his gratitude, and a sufficient proof of this was furnished by the presents which he left behind and which consisted of jewels, precious stones and pieces of embroidery.

Now Wilhelm too had completed his travel preparations and the company was all the more embarrassed that there was no news from the Doctor; they were afraid that a misfortune might have befallen the poor Harpist, just at the time when it was possible to hope that his condition could be very much improved. The courier was despatched, and he had hardly left before the Doctor arrived in the evening with a stranger whose appearance and personality were significant, serious and striking, and whom nobody knew. Both arrivals were quiet for a time; finally the stranger went up to Wilhelm, held out his hand to him and said, 'Don't you know your old friend any more?' It was the

Harpist's voice, but no trace of his former presence seemed to have remained. He was in the usual attire of a traveller, was cleanly and respectably dressed, his beard had gone, his hair had been dressed with some care, and what in fact made him quite unrecognizable was that there was no longer any traces of ageing to be seen in his significantly expressive features. Wilhelm embraced him with animation and joy; he was introduced to the others and behaved very sensibly, not knowing how familiar he had become to the company only a little time before. 'You will be patient with someone,' he continued with great composure, 'who, however adult he may appear, is like an inexperienced child as he appears before the world after a long illness. I owe it to this excellent man that I can appear in human society again.'

He was welcomed, and the Doctor immediately arranged a walk, in order to break off the conversation and to steer it into uncontroversial channels.

When they were on their own the Doctor gave the following explanation: 'Our success with the curing of this man is due to the strangest chance. We had been treating him for a long time according to our convictions, both mentally and physically, things went quite well to a certain extent too, but he was still much beset by the fear of death and he refused to sacrifice his beard and long cloak for us; what is more, he took more notice of things in the world, and his songs, like his imagination, seemed to be drawing nearer to life again. You know how a strange letter from the priest called me away from here. I came and found that our man was completely changed, he had let his hair be dressed in the customary fashion, he asked for ordinary clothes and seemed all at once to have become another person. We were curious to find out the reason for this transformation, and yet we did not venture to go into the subject with him directly; finally we chanced to discover the strange circumstances. A glass of liquid opium was missing from the priest's medicine-chest, it was considered necessary to mount the strictest search, everyone endeavoured to avoid suspicion, there were impassioned scenes among members of the household. In the end the man appeared and confessed that he had it; he was asked if he had taken any of it. He said "no", but went on: "It is to this possession that I owe the return of my reason. If you take the step of removing this phial from me, you will see me relapse without hope into my old condition. The feeling that it was desirable to see the sufferings of this world first of all led me to the path of recovery; soon after that, the thought occurred to me of ending these ills by taking my own life, and it was with this purpose that I removed the phial; the means of at once removing for ever the great grief gave me the strength to bear the suffering, and so, since possessing this talisman, I have urged myself back to life again because of the proximity of death. Don't fear that I may make use of it," he said, "but decide, as people with knowledge of the human heart, that you will really make me dependent on life by conceding to me independence from life." After mature reflection we did not press him further, and now he carries about with him in a firm, polished phial this poison as a most unusual antidote.'

The Doctor was informed about everything that had been discovered in the meantime, and it was decided to observe the strictest silence towards Augustine. The Abbé resolved not to let him out of sight and to lead him further along the righteous path that he had taken.

Meanwhile it was being arranged that Wilhelm should complete the journey through Germany with the Marchese. If it seemed possible to instil once more into Augustine a liking for his mother-country, it was planned to reveal this situation to his relatives, and Wilhelm was to lead him again to his own people.

Wilhelm had now made all the preparations for his journey, and if at first it seemed strange that Augustine should be pleased on hearing that his old friend and benefactor was at once to be leaving again, the Abbé soon discovered the reason for this strange emotional reaction. Augustine was unable to overcome his old fear of Felix and wanted to see the boy out of the way, the sooner the better.

Now gradually so many people had arrived that is was difficult to accommodate them all in the castle and its annexes, all the more so as they had not at first made arrangements to receive so many guests. They took breakfast and dined together, and would have gladly convinced themselves that they were living in agreeable harmony, even if on the quiet individuals longed to be apart from each other, so to speak. Theresa had gone riding with Lothario a number of times, even more frequently on her own, she had already met all the farmers and their wives in the neighbourhood; it was her principle in keeping house, and she might well have been right, that one should be on the best of terms with neighbours and always be involved in exchanges of hospitality. There did not seem to be any talk of a union between her and Lothario, the two sisters had a lot to say to each other, the Abbé seemed to be seeking the Harpist's company, Jarno was often in conference with the Doctor, Friedrich stayed close to Wilhelm, and Felix was everywhere where things went well for him. In this way the couples mostly came together for walks, where the group was separated, and when the company did have to be together they hastily escaped into the realm of music, for in music all could be united while at the same time each one could regain himself.

Unexpectedly the Count added to the numbers when he came to collect his wife and, as it seemed, to take leave formally from his relations in the world Jarno hurried to meet him as his coach arrived, and when the new arrival asked what sort of company was there, the former was overcome by the crazy mood which always seized hold of him when he caught sight of the Count and said: 'You will find the whole aristocracy of the world collected here, Marchesi, Marquis, Mylords and Barons, all that was missing was a Count.' So they went up the steps, and Wilhelm was the first person whom the Count met in the entrance hall. 'Mylord!' the Count said to him in French, after looking at him for a moment, 'I am very pleased to renew your acquaintance unexpectedly; for unless I am very much mistaken, I saw you in attendance on the Prince in my castle.'—'I did have the good fortune to attend on your Excellency at that time,' Wilhelm rejoined, 'only you were honouring me too much by taking me for an Englishman, and what is more one from the topmost rank, I am a German, and—' 'Certainly a very worthy young man,' Jarno at once interposed. The Count looked at Wilhelm with a smile and was about to make some reply, when the rest of the company came along and welcomed him in the most friendly manner. There were apologies that they could not immediately designate a decent room for him, and promises to procure the necessary accommodation straightaway.

'Aha!' he said with a smile, 'I can see that chance has been allowed to prepare the quartermaster's list. How much is not possible with the exercise of foresight and adjustment! Now I beg of you, let not a slipper be moved from its place on my account, for otherwise, I can see, there will be a great disarray. Everybody will be housed uncomfortably, and nobody should suffer that for my sake, not even for an hour, if it can be helped. You were a witness,' he said to Jarno, 'and you too, sir,' as he turned to Wilhelm, 'as to how many people I put up in comfort in my castle that time. If I'm provided with the list of people and servants and am shown how everybody is accommodated at present, I will make a re-allocation plan, so that everyone will have spacious quarters with the least trouble and that there should still be room for a visitor who might arrive by chance.'

Jarno at once took the part of adjutant to the Count, provided him with all the necessary papers, and in his own way had the greatest fun if he could mislead the old gentleman now and then. The latter, however, soon enjoyed a great triumph. The arrangements were complete, he had the names written above all the doors in his presence, and it could not be denied that the purpose had been completely achieved with little fuss and few changes. Furthermore, Jarno had arranged among other things that those people who at the present moment had common interests should be near to one another.

After all these arrangements had been made, the Count said to Jarno: 'Help me to place the young man you call Meister and who is supposed to be a German.' Jarno kept silent, for he knew full well that the Count was one of those people who, when they ask a question, actually want to give instruction; the latter too, without waiting for an answer, continued in his discourse: 'On that previous occasion you had introduced him to me and recommended him highly in the name of the Prince. Even if his mother was a German, I would guarantee that his father's an Englishman, and of good family too; who could keep account of all the British blood that has been flowing around in German veins for the last thirty years! I won't press any further, you always have such family secrets; but in this sort of instance you won't put anything across on me.' Then he related various things that were supposed to have happened at his castle that time, involving Wilhelm; Jarno likewise kept silent at this, although the Count was completely in error and more than once confused Wilhelm with a young Englishman in the Prince's entourage. Formerly the good gentleman had had an excellent memory, and he was still proud of being able to remember the most trivial circumstances of his youth; but now he was equally certain in pronouncing as true strange conjectures and fables which his imagination had on occasion deluded him with as his weakness of memory increased. What is more, he had become very gentle and agreeable, and his presence had a really favourable influence on the company. He asked that they should read something profitable together, indeed he even occasionally introduced little games which he organized with great care, though without joining in, and when people expressed surprise at his condescension, he said that it was the duty of anyone who was removing himself from the world in matters of significance to put himself on the same level as the world in unimportant things.

In the course of these games Wilhelm had more than one anxious and irritating moment; the frivolous Friedrich took the opportunity on more than one occasion of indicating Wilhelm's fondness for Natalie. How could this occur to him? What justification did he have? And would not the company believe that, since the two of them were much together, Wilhelm had confided in him in an incautious and unfortunate manner?

One day they were more light-hearted than usual with a joke on these lines when all at once Augustine wrenched open the door and rushed in with an appearance that was shocking; his face was pale, his eyes wild, he seemed to be trying to speak, speech failed him. The company was alarmed, Lothario and Jarno, thinking that there might be a return of his insanity, leapt towards him and held him fast. Firstly stammering and in a muffled manner, then with wild emphasis, he spoke and cried out: 'Don't hold me, hurry! Help! Do something to save the child! Felix has been poisoned!'

They let him go, he hurried out by the door, and the others hastened after him, full of alarm. The Doctor was summoned, Augustine went in the direction of the Abbé's room, they found the child, who appeared terrified and embarrassed when they called to him before reaching him, asking: 'What have you been up to?'

'Dear father,' Felix cried, 'I didn't drink from the bottle, I drank from the glass, I was so thirsty.'

Augustine clapped his hands together, calling out: 'He's lost!', then pushed his way through the group standing around and hurried away.

They found a glass of almond milk on the table and nearby a carafe that was more than half empty; the Doctor came, listened to what had happened, and was horrified to see the well-known phial, which had contained the liquid opium, lying empty on the table; he had vinegar brought along and summoned the help of all the means of his profession.

Natalie had the boy taken into one of the rooms and tended him anxiously. The Abbé had rushed off to find Augustine and to demand some explanation from him. The unhappy father had made vain attempts with a similar end in view and when he came back, he saw anxiety and worry on all faces. Meanwhile the Doctor had examined the almond milk in the glass, a very strong admixture of opium was found in it, the child lay on the sofa and seemed to be very ill, he begged his father to stop people from pouring stuff into him and tormenting him. Lothario had sent out his people and had set off on horseback himself in order to try to pursue Augustine. Natalie sat with the child, he took refuge on her lap and implored her for protection and for a lump of sugar, for the vinegar had been really too sour! The Doctor consented; the child, who was terribly agitated, should be allowed to rest for a moment, he said; everything advisable had been put into effect, he would do all that was possible. The Count came along, with some reluctance, as it appeared; he looked serious, indeed solemn, laid his hands on the child, looked up to heaven, and remained for some moments in this stance. Wilhelm who was sitting disconsolately in an armchair jumped up, cast a glance full of despair upon Natalie and went out of the door.

A little later the Count left the room too.

'I don't understand,' the Doctor said after a pause, 'why not the slightest trace of danger appears in the condition of the child. Even with only one gulp he must have taken a massive dose of opium, and now I can detect no further movement of his pulse than what I can ascribe to my own treatment and to the fear which we have induced in the child.'

Soon afterwards Jarno came in with the news that Augustine had been found lying in his own blood on the attic floor, there was a razor at his side, presumably he had cut his throat. The Doctor hurried off and met the people who were bringing the body downstairs. Augustine was laid upon a bed and examined thoroughly, the wound had penetrated the windpipe, unconsciousness had supervened after a severe loss of blood, but it soon became obvious that there was still life and hope. The Doctor arranged the body in the right position, joined the separated parts and applied a bandage. For all of them it was a sleepless and anxious night. The child refused to be separated from Natalie. Wilhelm sat on a stool in front of her; he had the boy's feet in his lap, while the child's head and chest lay in hers, and in this way they shared the pleasant burden and the grievous cares, waiting in this uncomfortable and sad position until daybreak; Natalie had given Wilhelm her hand, they said nothing, looked upon the child and looked at each other. Lothario and Jarno were seated at the other end of the room and were conducting a very serious conversation, which we would gladly share with our readers, if the course of events were not pressing upon us too urgently. The boy slept quietly, woke up cheerfully in the early morning, leapt up and asked for bread and butter.

As soon as Augustine had recovered to some extent, attempts were made to obtain some explanation from him. It was learnt, not without trouble and only gradually, that after he had been allocated a room with the Abbé because of the Count's unfortunate re-arrangement of accommodation, he had discovered the manuscript with his own story in it; his fright had been unparalleled, and he had now convinced himself that he was not to live any longer; he had at once had recourse, as usual, to the opium, had poured some into a glass of almond milk, but had none the less shuddered on putting it to his lips; he had then left it in order to walk through the garden once more and to see the world, on his return he had found the child occupied just then with filling up again the glass from which he had been drinking.

They begged the unfortunate man to be quiet, he grasped Wilhelm convulsively by the hand, saying, 'Oh, why didn't I leave you long ago! For I knew that I would kill the boy, and he me.'— 'The boy is alive!', Wilhelm said. The Doctor, who had been listening attentively, asked Augustine if all the drink had been poisoned. 'No', he replied, 'only the glass.'—'So, by the happiest chance, the child drank out of the carafe! A guardian angel guided his hand so that it did not grasp towards the death that stood ready prepared so nearby!'—'No, no!' Wilhelm exclaimed with a cry, placing his hands before his eyes, 'what a terrible statement this is! The child said expressly that he didn't drink from the carafe, but the glass. His health is only an illusion, he will slip away and die quietly.' He hurried off, the Doctor bent down and fondled the child, saying, 'Now Felix, you had a drink from the carafe and not from the glass, didn't you?' The child started crying. The Doctor told Natalie quietly how matters stood; she too attempted in vain to elicit the truth from the child, he only wept the more copiously, and went on until he fell asleep.

Wilhelm kept watch at his side, the night passed quietly. The next morning Augustine was found dead in his bed; he had deceived the watchfulness of his attendants by an apparent calm, had quietly untied the bandage and bled to death. Natalie took the child for a walk, he was as cheerful as in his happiest times. 'You really are kind,' Felix said to her, 'you don't quarrel, you don't smack me, I will just tell you, I did drink from the carafe! Mother Aurelia always used to smack me on my fingers when I stretched out my hand for the carafe. Father looked so angry, I thought he would hit me.'

Natalie returned to the castle as if on wings, and Wilhelm, still full of anxiety, went out to meet her. 'Happy father!' she exclaimed, lifting up the child and handing him over to Wilhelm, 'here's your son! He drank out of the carafe, his bad manners have saved him.'

The happy outcome was related to the Count, who, however, only listened with that smiling, quiet, modest certainty with which one may tolerate the errors of good people. Jarno, alert about everything, could not this time explain such a high degree of complacency, until he finally learnt after many circumlocutions that the Count was convinced that the child had really taken poison, but that he had miraculously preserved his life by his prayers and by laying his hands on the child. He now also decided to go away immediately; as was usual with him, all his packing was complete in one moment, and as they were saying goodbye the beautiful Countess took hold of Wilhelm's hand before she let go her sister's, joined all four hands together, turned round quickly and got into the carriage.

A kind of feverish vibration had been brought into the household by so many terrible and amazing events which followed one on top of the other, forced people to an unusual way of life and introduced disorder and confusion everywhere. The hours of sleeping and waking, of eating, drinking and social gathering had been displaced and reversed. Apart from Theresa nobody had remained on his usual course; the men tried to restore their good spirits with strong drink and as they induced in themselves an artificial good humour, they banished the natural disposition which alone grants us true serenity and being.

Wilhelm had been moved and unsettled by the most vehement emotions; the unexpected and terrifying shocks had completely put his inner self into a position where it could not resist a passion that had so violently taken hold of his heart. Felix had been returned to him, and yet everything seemed to be wrong; the letters from Werner with the bills of exchange were there, he lacked nothing for his journey except the courage to depart. Everything was urging him on to this journey. He could surmise that Lothario and Theresa were only waiting for his departure in order to get married. Jarno was unusually quiet, and it could almost have been said that he had lost something of his usual cheerfulness. Fortunately the Doctor helped our friend out of his embarrassment to some extent by pronouncing him to be ill and giving him medicine.

The company always came together in the evening, and the boisterous Friedrich, who usually drank more wine than was reasonable, dominated the conversation and in his way made the group laugh with hundreds of quotations and joking allusions, and also not infrequently embarrassed them by permitting himself to think aloud.

He did not seem to believe in his friend's illness at all. Once, when they were all together, he called out: 'Doctor, what do you call the affliction that has beset our friend? Does none of the three thousand names with which you deck out your ignorance apply here? At least there has not been a lack of similar examples. An example of this type,' he continued with an emphatic smile, 'can be found in Egyptian or Babylonian history.'

The company looked at each other and smiled.

'What was the king's name?' he called out and paused for a moment. 'If you don't want to help me, I shall be able to help myself.' He pulled open the doors and pointed to the big picture in the entrance hall. 'What's the name of the goatee-bearded one with the crown over there who is pining away at the foot of the bed because of his sick son? What's the name of the beauty who is coming in and whose roguish eyes contain both poison and antidote? What's the name of the clumsy doctor who only sees the point at this very moment and who for the first time in his life has the opportunity to make out a sensible prescription and to hand over a medicament which provides a complete cure and which is as palatable as it is salutary?'

He went on showing off in this style. The company controlled themselves as well as possible and concealed their embarrassment behind forced smiles. Natalie's cheeks reddened a little and betrayed the agitation of her heart. Fortunately she was walking to and fro with Jarno; when she came to the door she shrewdly stepped outside, paced a few times up and down in the entrance hall, and then went to her room.

The company remained quiet. Friedrich began singing and dancing:

> Wonders you'll see face to face!
> What has happened has taken place,
> What's been spoken has been told,
> Before night's cold,
> You'll see wonders face to face.

Theresa had followed Natalie, Friedrich led the Doctor in front of the large painting, made a ridiculous speech in praise of medicine and slipped off.

Up to now Lothario had been standing in a window niche, and he was looking down into the garden without moving. Wilhelm was in the most terrible position. Even now that he realized that he was alone with his friend, he remained still for a time; he looked back fleetingly at his own story and finally contemplated with a shudder his present condition; in the end he jumped up and cried out: 'If I am to blame for what is taking place, and for what is happening to me and to you, then punish me! In addition to my other sorrows you deprive me of your friendship and let me go out without consolation into the wide world where I should have gone and lost myself long since. But if you see me as the victim of a cruel, chance entanglement from which I was incapable of escaping, give me the assurance of your love and friendship to take with me on a journey which I may no longer postpone. A time will come when I shall be able to tell you what has been taking place within me during recent days. Perhaps I am suffering this punishment at this present time because I did not reveal myself to you early enough, because I have hesitated to show myself to you completely as I am; you would have stood by me, you would have helped me to free myself at the right time. Time and time again my eyes are opened about myself, always too late and always in vain. How much I deserved Jarno's reprimand! How I thought that I had accepted it, how I hoped to make use of it and to gain a new life! Could I? Should I? It is in vain that we human beings accuse ourselves and accuse Fate! We are wretched and are destined to wretchedness, and is it not a matter of complete indifference whether our own guilt, a higher influence or chance, virtue or vice, wisdom or madness hurl us to destruction? Farewell! I will stay no longer in the house in which I have offended so terribly, and against my will, against the laws of hospitality. Your brother's indiscretion is unpardonable, it intensifies my unhappiness to an extreme degree, it makes me despair.'

'And if now,' Lothario replied, taking his hand, 'your union with my sister were the secret condition upon which Theresa has resolved to give me her hand? A recompense of this nature is what the fine girl has intended for you; she vowed that these two couples should go to the altar on *one* day. "His reason chose me," she said, "his heart asks for Natalie, and my reason will come to the help of his heart." We agreed to observe Natalie and yourself, we took the Abbé into our confidence, and had to promise him not to take any step that might further this union, but to let everything take its natural course. This is what we have done. Nature did take her course, and all the crazy brother has done is to shake down the ripe fruit. Now that we have come together in this amazing way, let us not lead commonplace lives; let us live in a worthwhile way! It is incredible what a cultivated man can do for himself and others if, without wishing to rule, he has a mind to be the guardian of many, and if he guides them to do at the right time what they would really all like to be doing, and leads them to the fulfilment of their own purposes which for the most part they keep well in view, though they only miss the paths to take them there. Let us form an alliance with this concern in mind! It is no illusion, it's an idea that is really quite practicable and one that is often put into practice by good people, though not always with conscious awareness. My sister Natalie is a clear example of this. The mode of action which nature has prescribed for this beautiful soul will always be unattainable. Indeed, she rather than many others deserves this name of honour, more, if I may say so, than our noble aunt herself who had the most beautiful nature that we knew in our circle at the time when our good doctor was editing that manuscript. Since then Natalie has been developing, and everyone is happy as she now is.'

He wanted to continue, but Friedrich rushed in with a lot of noise. 'What sort of wreath do I deserve?' he called out, 'and how are you going to reward me? Bind together myrtle, laurel, ivy, oak-leaves, the greenest you can find; there are so many merits in me that you have to crown. Natalie is yours! I am the magician who has raised up this treasure.'

'He's raving,' said Wilhelm, 'and I'm going.'

'Have you got a message?' the Baron said, holding on to Wilhelm.

'In my own power and authority,' Friedrich replied, 'also by the grace of God, if you like; just as I was acting on behalf of the wooer, so now I am an ambassador, I've been listening at the keyhole, she has told her whole story to the Abbé.'

'You shameless fellow!' Lothario said, 'who told you to eavesdrop?'

'Who told her to shut herself away!' Friedrich rejoined; 'I heard everything quite distinctly, Natalie was very upset. During the night when the child seemed to be so ill and was half lying in her lap, while you sat disconsolately before her and shared the precious burden with her, she vowed that if the child should die, she would confess her love to you and offer you her hand herself; now that the child is living, why should she change her attitude? A promise that has been made under such circumstances is one that is kept under all conditions. Now the parson will come along and will be full of himself at all the news he is bringing.'

The Abbé entered the room. 'We know everything,' Friedrich called out to him as he approached, 'make it short, for you're coming here merely as a matter of form, that's the only reason why the gentlemen are wanted.'

'He's been eavesdropping,' the Baron said.—'What bad breeding!' the Abbé cried.

'Quickly now!' Friedrich went on, 'how about the ceremonies? They can be counted on your fingers, you must travel, the Marchese's invitation fits in wonderfully for you. Once you are over the Alps, everything will sort itself out at home, people will be grateful to you if you undertake something out of the ordinary, you'll provide them with an entertainment that they don't need to pay for. It's just as if you were giving a public fancy-dress ball; all social classes can take part.'

'It's true, you've already made yourself serviceable to the public with such popular celebrations,' the Abbé replied, 'and it looks as if I'm not going to be able to say a word today.'

'If it's not all as I say,' Friedrich rejoined, 'correct us! Come on over, come on over! We must have a look at them and rejoice.'

Lothario embraced his friend and led him to his sister; she came towards him with Theresa; everyone was silent.

'No dallying!' Friedrich exclaimed. 'In two days you can be ready to travel. What do you think, my friend,' he continued, turning to Wilhelm, 'when we first met, when I asked you for the pretty bunch of flowers, who could imagine that you would ever receive a flower like this from my hand?'

'Don't remind me of those times at this moment of supreme happiness!'

'You shouldn't be ashamed of them, any more than people should be ashamed of their origins. They were good times, I can't help laughing when I look at you: you seem to me to be like Saul, the son of Kish, who went out to look for his father's asses and found a kingdom.'

'I don't know what a kingdom is worth,' Wilhelm replied, 'but I do know that I have attained a happiness which I don't deserve and which I would not like to exchange for anything in the world.'

Acknowledgments

I should like to express here my appreciation of the help given to me by Mrs. Yvette Millard who prepared the typescript of this translation, and by Agnes Rook with her thoughtful suggestions in connection with the final draft.—H.M.W.

Principal Dates of Goethe's Life

1749	Born at Frankfurt am Main
1765	Studied at Leipzig
1770-71	Studied law at Strassburg
1772	Spent some months in Wetzlar at the supreme court of the Empire
1773	*Götz von Berlichingen* (prose drama)
1774	*Clavigo* (prose drama)
1774	*Die Leiden des jungen Werthers* (novel)
1775	Becomes companion to the young Duke Karl August at Weimar and subsequently becomes much involved in administrative work there.
1786-88	Journey to Italy
1787	*Iphigenie auf Tauris* (verse drama)
1788	*Egmont* (prose drama)
1788	After returning to Weimar from Italy, beginning of relationship with Christiane Vulpius.
1789	*Torquato Tasso* (verse drama)
	Birth of August, son of Goethe and Christiane.
1790	*Faust. Ein Fragment* (verse drama)
1791	Becomes artistic director of the Weimar court theatre, remaining in this office until 1817.
1792-93	Accompanies the Duke Karl August on campaign against France.
1795	*Unterhaltungen deutscher Ausgewanderten* (prose fiction)
1795	*Römische Elegien* (cycle of poems)
1795-96	*Wilhelm Meisters Lehrjahre* (novel)
1797	*Hermann und Dorothea* (verse epic)
1803	*Die natürliche Tochter* (verse drama)
1806	Marriage to Christiane
1808	*Faust. Erster Teil* (verse drama)
1809	*Die Wahlverwandtschaften* (novel)
1809	*Pandora* (masque in verse)
1811-33	*Dichtung und Wahrheit* (autobiography)
1816	Death of Christiane
1816-17	*Italienische Reise* (autobiography)
1819	*West-östlicher Divan* (cycle of poems)
1828	*Novelle* (prose fiction)
1829	*Wilhelm Meisters Wanderjahre* (final version of the second part of the novel)
1832	Death of Goethe
1833	*Faust. Der Tragödie zweiter Teil* (verse drama)